Precious Scars

My Journey to Freedom
through Forgiveness

Sara and Judy —
Thank you for your
friendship —
Yehuda

YEHUDA JACOBI

Precious Scars
My Journey to Freedom through Forgiveness

© 2013 by Yehuda Jacobi

ISBN 0991034821
ISBN 13 9780991034826

Library of Congress Control Number: 2013919575
Cover design by CreateSpace
Back cover and Afterword photos by Julie Kaplan Photography
Chapter heading Hebrew translations by Rakefet Richmond

Published by
Chazak Press
P.O. Box 527
Morton Grove, IL 60053

Printed in the United States of America

Table of Contents

For Michael

Like Noah, I was in one world, but you brought me into another, one with a rainbow. You are my companion, my best friend, my bashert.

Acknowledgments

Although this is my story, I know I couldn't tell it without the assistance and input of many friends who have generously given me their valuable time. I want to thank Alan Tony Amberg, Jonathan Edelman, Elizabeth Gillies, and Michael Thompson for reviewing this manuscript, fielding my countless questions, and extending their support and encouragement. Special thanks to Beth Snyder, who stood by me in this endeavor and was an inspiration to me during the times when I wanted to give up.

Thank you to family members Karen Berg-Raftakis and Richard J. DeLuca for their review. Thank you to Rabbi Cindy Enger, Rabbi Evan Moffic, Matt Santori-Griffith, Matt Simonette, Chip Smith, Diane Warren, and Lynn Allyn Young for their advice.

A special note of appreciation to Rev. Christine Chakoian, Carole Devine, Rabbi Laurence Edwards, Rabbi Suzanne Griffel, and Malcolm Westfield for their presence and support over the years.

Finally, I am grateful for the guidance of Arthur, Dr. Edwin Martin, and, of course, my mom and dad, all of whom still provide assistance in spirit.

Author's Note

The names and other identifying details of some of the people in this book have been changed. Any slights of people or organizations are unintentional. My siblings have expressed the desire to have their privacy protected so the reader will see very few references to them and then only in general terms.

I don't view God as being one gender or another. Actually, I conceive of God as being beyond gender. For simplicity's sake, I refer to God in this text as male.

"The rabbi" is a fictional character I created and have used throughout the text. I intend to use this character to express teachings I learned from various Kabbalah classes and seminars.

Introduction

Our first teacher is our own heart.
Cheyenne Proverb

The Rev. Christine Chakoian, pastor of the prestigious First Presbyterian Church of Lake Forest, Illinois, once told me, "Preachers always run the risk of getting too familiar. Most don't cross a certain line. However, there are certain stories that require telling."[1] While I am not a minister or a rabbi, I do have a story to tell.

Today, information about one another flows freely, and people share themselves openly in personal life and in digital media. I am uncomfortable with the notion of sharing my story, since to do so I would have to reveal my intellectual and emotional struggles in order to illustrate the concepts within this book. I am all too aware of maintaining proper boundaries, and by sharing too much I would only impair the boundaries I have tried so hard to establish as an adult. However, it may be that the only way to communicate what I have to say is to "cross that certain line," as Rev. Chakoian states. Therefore, I have chosen to open my heart to make myself visible and vulnerable for the reader in order to write more effectively. As a result, some of the material is emotionally raw, perhaps intense, but it is honest.

This book is a collection of spiritual discoveries I made while struggling to work through my childhood abuse. Ultimately, the story I tell is how I learned to confront, forgive, and heal my life's distortions, or my erroneous beliefs and assumptions about my parents. My lesson was to transform those distortions and rise above the abuse. If I could not learn to do this, I would eternally be a victim. With each discovery, I hope to establish a movement within the material from Darkness to Light.

I have strongly resisted using the words *childhood abuse* in the title of this book, and it is not my intent for the book itself to be a "tell-all"

book in the sensational sense of the words. Although abuse is the framework for the stories I tell, the larger and more important story is the spiritual perspective I developed during those years of physical and emotional pain. This perspective does not tie itself to any one religion or thought system, but instead encompasses all of them, in one way or another.

A few comments about the content of the material might be helpful. The most significant point to mention is the use of dreams within the text. I have always been a dreamer with vivid recall. Born under the astrological sign of Pisces, I think it is easier for me to dance in the dream world than simply walk in this physical one. Dreams can be a fascinating tool for self-development. They represent keys to unlock closed doors that don't readily open through conscious methods. I hope that the reader will see how I used my dreams to guide me through the rough spots in my life.

Some pieces in the book are essays of varying length written in the memoir style; still others are modified *D'vrei* Torah[i] (literally "words of Torah," or to use the vernacular, a sermon) that I have delivered in our temple, Congregation Or Chadash, in Chicago, Illinois.

My upbringing was Christian, and I spent five years studying at a Roman Catholic seminary. I added to this knowledge when I studied Spiritualism at The Memorial Spiritualist Church in Norfolk, Virginia. I also had a private teacher, the late Rev. Cathy Mannino,

---

i The first five books of the Jewish Bible: Genesis, Exodus, Leviticus, Numbers, and Deuteronomy.

who taught me trance mediumship,[ii] sometimes called channeling. Some of the information in this book was channeled.

There are references to Eastern religions as well, reflecting my studies for eleven years with my late Taoist[iii] partner, Arthur. Many of Taoism's concepts align themselves harmoniously with Judaism. There was a natural transition for me to embrace Judaism because of the similarities in theological concepts.

Islam is not mentioned here. This is not a slight; I simply do not know anything about the religion, never having studied it. I do feel that all religions have something to offer: they are simply different perspectives for relating to God.

I also present relevant material from my journals. The biggest challenge in writing was using my daily and dream journals to show the psychological and emotional conflict and resolution of my life's events.

The reader will not find any answers here, just perspectives. Naturally, my perspectives changed when my awareness evolved and I altered the direction in which I traveled. It is possible these articles will challenge your belief system. If you let yourself engage with your feelings, these stories may evolve for you and lead you to

---

ii The process of delivering information in an altered state of consciousness, with or without the help of a spirit not incarnated on the physical plane. This term originated from the Spiritualist religion. Edgar Cayce and Jane Roberts are two individuals who were trance mediums, although it is my understanding that Ms. Roberts did not like or apply the term to herself.

iii A follower of Taoism. Taoism is a Chinese philosophical system that emphasizes discovering the energies of the world and living in harmony with them.

an understanding of where I have been. If one story does not elicit a reaction from you, perhaps the next one will. What is important is that the reader then has the responsibility to engage with his or her reaction. If that reaction stimulates awareness, the reader, in effect, becomes his or her own teacher. I do hope you will examine your reactions, whether positive or negative, to see where they will take you.

I deliberately wrote this book in the first person because, however cumbersome the style might be, I hoped to relay to the reader that this is my journey. If you identify with some of the footsteps I have taken, maybe my words can provide insight, clarity, or comfort. I view life as a journey that every soul must travel to learn its lessons. At this point in time, within these pages are the discoveries I have made on mine.

In The Beginning

Bereshit

Creation

No matter what happens to you, what you remember is up to you.
Matthew Buckley

⟋⟋⟋

I dreaded coming home from grade school. Dad worked the night shift downtown as a router for the REA Express (the predecessor of UPS), but if he decided to drink in the morning, I could count on him to be home, waiting for me. If he had passed out on the couch, I was safe. However, often he was just sitting, watching TV with his beer in hand.

Sometimes he wouldn't even acknowledge me. Other times he would just glare at me. I quickly learned to take care of my personal business and run to my room, where I could hide from him. If I was out of sight, my presence was less likely to antagonize him for whatever offense he decided I had committed that day. I was accustomed to his behavior but didn't understand why it had to be this way.

My maternal grandmother pulled me aside every now and then to reassure me I had done nothing wrong. She said, "It's a sickness, honey. Your father can't help himself." Grandma's explanations, while sincere, were of no help as my child mind struggled to understand why my father was different from other fathers and why no one helped him. If it was a sickness, why didn't they take him to a doctor who could make him well? Yet, heaven forbid that I talked about it. "It" was my father's alcoholism and cast a shadow on anything we did outside of the home. Why was I not allowed to talk about "It?" Why all the secrecy?

My friends had neat fathers who took their kids to fun places like Kiddieland, a popular amusement park in the fifties and sixties. Many times, Dad had promised that he, too, would take the whole family there on a Sunday afternoon. Then he would start drinking, and his promises never materialized. Let me amend that: there was one time when he did take us all. All those other times, I would fantasize about my friends' dads being my own, and about all the happy times we would have had. Any of these other fathers would have done, as they all were happy and treated their kids well. The father I wanted would have been good to me and supportive of me. My father was critical and demanding, as well as emotionally, verbally, and physically abusive.

There were times when he was a loving father who encouraged me to run to him and trust him, until the next liquor-fueled incident, after which I ran away from him again and shut down or withdrew. His inconsistent behavior only made me distrust him. Anxiety accompanied my distrust, since I never knew what to expect from him. One day he returned home from work with a Beatles magazine in hand. When he saw someone had left it behind at work, he thought of me and picked it up. He knew I liked the Beatles. I was thrilled with the attention. The next day I bought a different Beatles magazine. It was $1.50. When he returned home from work, I ran to him to show him what I had bought. He promptly blew up at me, telling me I was a fool for wasting my allowance on that "nonsense." Mom called his two personalities Dr. Jekyll and Mr. Hyde, so dramatic was the change, particularly when he drank. I never felt safe with him.

When the verbal abuse wasn't enough, he would slap my face. He seemed to like doing that. When I was ten, there was a day when he wasn't content with just slapping me. He started hitting me until I ran into my bedroom to escape him, my mother following behind, trying to stop him. I was on the bed against the corner of the wall, and he dragged me back to him and continued to hit me. I only recovered this memory in therapy, learning that I had repressed this and other memories out of a need to survive the abuse.

The second child of four, I was the second son. They had wanted a girl but she arrived five years later, and five years after that, my younger brother joined us. My experiences with Mom and Dad were different from my siblings because of our age differences when the abuse started. The abuse escalated with the passage of time, and by then my older brother was out of the house, off to college. My childhood illnesses only aggravated an already fearful situation.

Growing up, I viewed my older brother as better than me since Dad seemed to treat him more favorably, but then turn around and use my face as a punching bag. Slapping my face was an assault to my pride and dignity. With no "face" to show to the world, I felt I had no value. What was wrong with me?

My anger with Dad grew internally while I cowered in his presence and avoided him when I could. I didn't really stand up to him until I reached my teens, the time when everyone starts challenging their authority figures, starting with their parents. As I grew older (and physically stronger), my anger morphed into rage; he sensed my growing strength and hesitated to slap me. Even as the frequency of his hitting decreased, our arguments increased. In all of those arguments, I was "good for nothing," a term he liked to throw at me. The volume of our fighting rose and spilled out of the house at times, to within earshot of the neighbors, who, of course, commented to Mom when she returned from work.

I felt bad for Mom. Seeing the bare refrigerator, particularly at the end of the month, I worried about all the money going to liquor and that there would be no more food. Grandma helped us out, as she often just happened to have "extra" since there was a sale that week. I got used to shopping at Grandma's "store," and I am sure Mom was relieved she could do so, even though she protested. She must have felt guilty at times.

Seeing my parents fight, and not being able to talk about it, did not help me to relax and enjoy my childhood. I grew up too fast, which destroyed my innocence. Mom would complain to me, confide in me about Dad, not realizing she was making me her surrogate husband. As a result, she violated my personal boundaries as a child, just as Dad did, but in a different manner. My perception wasn't acute enough to understand that besides enabling Dad, she was failing to protect me. I only saw Mom as the victim and Dad as the villain.

Shortly after I graduated from college, after one argument too many, I abruptly left home for a dilapidated room in a boarding house. I departed in anger, thinking a physical departure would solve my problems. While a physical move did help, and I was able to sleep well for the first time in years, my issues accompanied me. They resided in a mental suitcase I carried along with the physical ones I left the house with. It was a suitcase filled with impaired boundaries, low self-worth, invalidated feelings, denial of my sexuality, guilt, fear, and most of all, the shame of simply being. I had to unpack, confront, and heal from all of these issues so I could function effectively as an individual. The weight of my issues held me back from any forward movement in life. I blamed my father for this, telling anyone who would listen how he scarred my childhood.

Marianne Williamson, in her lectures in her book *Forgiving Your Parents*, stated, "The parents are the primary image of the adult male and female. If parental roles are not supportive and affirmative to the child, the child grows up viewing life through a distorted lens."[2] My distorted vision presented an erroneous picture of who I was supposed to be as an adult male. These patterns of abuse would only repeat themselves unless I did something to address the issues.

Williamson also quoted *A Course in Miracles*, which describes not a religion but a thought system, and says that one is responsible for their perception of what happens.[3] With that idea in mind, I started to examine my perceptions, confront my feelings, and (eventually) release my attachment to how I expected my life to be. I could then view my life through a clearer lens of love and forgiveness.

Confronting my pain, over time, helped me understand that my parents were the perfect parents, exactly the parents with whom I should have been. How could that be true, considering how I just described them? It took some time, but I learned to view my "scarred childhood" as a teacher of experience. The individual scars (impaired boundaries, low self-worth, etc.) were all different

lessons. Scars are a tougher kind of tissue, a very real physical symbol of the toughness I needed to adopt in order to survive. While I didn't know it at the time, I learned that the soul creates its challenges on the physical level in the most effective way it can learn. I learned to use each physical event, no matter how devastating, to teach me. So, these scars became precious since I learned from them. They formed the basis for the following life experiences.

The First Step

The Lord is my Shepherd and He knows I'm Gay.
Rev. Troy Perry

⌒

I don't have many memories of life in my twenties. Part of the reason for the memory loss was trauma. Learning it was not safe to express myself at home; I dissociated from my experiences and shut down my emotions. I simply wasn't consciously there most of that time. While most young men at that age eagerly pursued their personal and professional goals, I muddled through life in a fog, not knowing what I wanted. I had studied five years in a Catholic seminary and loved the life there, yet I left because I realized it wasn't for me, for several reasons. One of those reasons was my sexuality.

The denial of my sexuality presented the biggest challenge to me. There was no one with whom I could share my feelings—not that I would even be able to share anything so intimate about myself

9

at that time. As a result, my isolation from everyone else was suffocating and frightening. There were no social outlets I knew of where I could meet people like me. There was no one in my world that seemed to feel like I did. There seemed to be no place in this world for me, and God, if there was one (by this time I wasn't sure), had played some cruel trick on me. I just couldn't conceive of continuing to live in this world with the feelings I had, feelings that, according to my religion, were sinful and darkened my soul. If the word *gay* was in use at that time I wasn't aware of it, but there certainly wasn't anything gay about my life then. I felt isolated, scared, and ashamed.

According to a letter I received from the GLBT National Help Center, in San Francisco, CA, a fifteen-year-old boy named Ryan described how "every day on the way home, he would walk to the middle of a bridge, look way down into the water, and decide whether that should be the day that he jumps."[4] I could identify with Ryan's contemplation of suicide. Tired of feeling alone and crying myself to sleep every night, I considered suicide over a period of two years. My desire for it was strong, and the thought of physically ending my existence, was to be frank, overwhelming. That idea stayed with me after I graduated from college. I delayed taking any action because, quite honestly, I couldn't think of the best way to do it.

There must have been a stronger impulse within me to continue living. This impulse accompanied my suicidal bent and it said, "Go to church." That made no sense, as I had left the church at the same time I left the seminary. I tried to dismiss the feeling, but it was as strong as my desire to do away with myself. I did hear about this place called Metropolitan Community Church on Wellington in Chicago, a church that the Rev. Troy Perry founded in 1968, welcoming all gay and lesbian individuals. I hardly ever ventured into Chicago, as I was never good with directions because I was afraid of getting lost (I explain the source of this fear in another essay, "Dwellers on the Threshold"). Already in my midtwenties, I felt like a scared little boy, but I somehow managed to find my way to the church. When I arrived, I met people who welcomed me. I felt I belonged there. I didn't know it at the time, but I had reached the end of one journey and begun another.

Abraham faced a similar journey. In Genesis chapter 12, verse 1, God challenges Abraham: "Go forth from your native land and from your father's house to the land that I will show you...and I will bless you."[5] Abraham leaves the land, along with his wife, Sarah, to travel where God leads them. A midrash[iv] for the Torah portion *Lech Lecha* interprets God as actually saying, "Go forth to find your authentic self, to learn who you are meant to be."[6] It can also mean, "Go to yourself." What Abraham had not done was to create a space within himself for the journey, because he was too self-absorbed. After all, he asked Sarah to lie to the Pharaoh by saying she was Abraham's sister. He literally put her life and virtue at risk.

In a similar manner, there could be no way for my journey to start because I could not move beyond my self-absorption with what religion and society taught me. Religion bombarded me with its version of the Ten Commandments: thou shalt be this race, sex, or sexual orientation. Society told me, in its own way, not who I was meant to be, but who I was expected to be.

---

iv Rabbinic commentary on the Hebrew Scriptures.

God could not help Abraham until he made the first step to move within. Once he took that first step, his life and his journey unfolded before him, taking him closer to God and fulfilling the purpose intended for him. No one else could open the closet door but me, but once I took that first step, my world unfolded in the same manner as Abraham's, with God there to support me. The point at which I transformed myself depended on my state of being, my ability to say to God, "*Hineini*" (Hebrew for "I am here"). I needed to be able to say, "I am here, I am fully present." I demonstrated that affirmation when I made an effort to override my fear and drive to the church that night.

One evening after services, I walked downstairs for the coffee hour, and there on the piano bench was a man named Arthur. He was a Taoist, but he studied all religions, particularly Eastern religion. I never heard the term "Taoist" before. We talked all night and for the next eleven years. He became my Teacher and laid a foundation that formed the basis for where I am now. I came to understand that the God who created me continues to lead and protect me on the journey I am making. God has always been with me, and God will certainly remain with me. When I can change my state of being to living in the present moment is when I begin to *know* it.

My ability to approach God is proportional to how well I embrace the holiness within myself, a holiness that emanates from God. When I begin with self-affirmation, there is no separation from Him; there is no isolation from Him. Fear, shame, and self-loathing simply cannot exist. I didn't know it then, but the night I went to church was my first step on the road to healing.

Boundaries

⌒

Gvoolot

When You Take

Without boundaries, a person has no protection.
John Bradshaw

⟨━━━⟩

The Torah portion *Ki Teitzei* appears to be a loose collection of laws, some obvious, some obscure, and some more applicable to past generations, but a common thread actually ties them all together. The Aramaic root of *Ki Teitzei* actually means "to connect." So what is the connection that holds these laws together, and what is the connection to me today?

One law mandates that anyone who builds a new house shall construct a fence around the roof, to prevent anyone from falling from it. The roofs of houses were flat in those days and used for socializing and sleeping in warm weather. This law implements a boundary to prevent harm to another person and is probably one of the first building codes.

A group of laws makes a provision for the orphan, the homeless, and the widow. These laws state that when harvesting your fields you must leave some of the harvest for those less fortunate. This law is a code of conduct that implements a boundary by which a person must provide for those less fortunate.

The translation of *Ki Teitzei is* "when you go out" or "when you wage war;" however, I have seen it phrased in the Etz Hayim[v] translation as "when you take."[7] I prefer the translation "when you take," because if you use those words and add the individual laws, the proper separation of boundaries is emphasized.

For example, when you take liberties with the safety of those who are on your property and do not build a fence around your roof, you have crossed a boundary and violated it. When you take the crops you should leave for those less fortunate, you have crossed a boundary and violated it.

These rules on the surface seem so small and innocuous, but boundaries are the connection that holds the laws together. The boundaries form the lines of respect and proper conduct of people toward one another. I think this Torah portion gently teaches the boundaries within which we need to behave. Can you imagine a world in which these boundaries are not in place? If there were no rules that told us to provide for the homeless, the widowed, and the orphaned, would organizations like The Ark[vi] or Habitat for Humanity exist? What would our society look like,

---

v Literally "Tree of Life."

vi A nonprofit organization in Chicago that provides food, shelter, medical, and legal services to Chicagoland Jews.

since many of the values society embraces find their roots in the Scriptures?

Women (and men) who have had their boundaries violated through abuse or oppression have a special challenge in that we do not have a clear comprehension of our identity. It is too easy to live for others rather than to assert our right to respect and self-determination.

Pia Mellody, a Senior Clinical Advisor at The Meadows, a clinic for trauma and addiction treatment in Wickenburg, Arizona, is a respected authority and leader in the field of child abuse and the trauma that develops from it. She has written several groundbreaking books on codependency, citing the lack of boundaries this condition generates.

She states in her book *Facing Codependence* that while infants and young children need to be hugged and kissed and cuddled to infuse them with a sense of their being loved and wanted, i.e., their own value, there is a time when that needs to stop. After a certain age, usually in upper-middle or high school age, she recommends refraining from physical contact and teaching the child that their body is their own, and that they alone determine who will touch their person. Pia would refrain from hugging her own son in this manner and would take cues for permission to have physical contact with him, or connect with him by talking to him. She was trying to teach him that the power to set boundaries resides with him and does not come from others.[8] I formed a few rules for myself based on Pia's teachings and the ones in *Ki Teitzei*.

When you hit me, you have violated my physical boundaries, damaging my body. Each slap also damages my spirit and generates shame. When you take the respect I am entitled to as a human being, you have crossed my boundaries, diminishing me as a person. I am more aware now, as an adult, when someone touches me without permission, for he or she takes my right to be in charge of my person. On the other hand, I am more aware of whether it is permissible to hug someone. If I don't get the cues it is okay to do so, I pull back, even at the risk of others perceiving me as aloof. I need to respect others' rights to their boundaries just as much I want them to respect mine.

Looking back, sometimes my behavior was inconsistent. As an example, I successfully told one person who was standing far too close to me to please step back. More recently, another individual had a habit of touching my shoulder or hugging me without my permission. Her gestures were startling, so I had difficulty affirming my boundaries by telling her not to touch me. I went from one extreme to the other, until I eventually learned to create a healthy, balanced presentation of myself.

When I share too much information with people I hardly know, I violate my own internal boundaries, boundaries that require a healthier separation between others and me. I have a right to decide how much to share, but too often can't ascertain when enough is enough. It takes a conscious effort. It takes trial and error.

These inconsistencies arose from my inability to declare who I am without feeling guilty about it. Whether the boundaries were internal or external, often what I thought were boundaries were really walls of anger. I achieved what I wanted but not without generating pain in others. As my self-image strengthened, my guilt dissipated. The boundaries are mine to set, and I learned to set the terms without feeling anxious about it. Even if there is limited success to my efforts, at least now I am aware of what is happening. Being aware is a good starting point for the eventual growth I want to achieve. Being aware, even if I am aware of something negative, means that my consciousness is changing.

Confrontation

~

Imutim

Dwellers on the Threshold

I will walk out of the Darkness and I'll walk into the Light…
Van Morrison

⟨ornament⟩

Years ago, I contacted our local cemetery to preplan my funeral. I met the sales representative, William, an elderly man who proceeded to familiarize himself with my burial needs. He delivered the preliminary sales talk that I expected. He mentioned how young I was, asked what did I do for a living, etc., and the conversation eventually drifted to family. He said he had no family, as they had all died in the Holocaust. At that time, Steven Spielberg was just starting his Holocaust Testimonials program, and I encouraged him to tell his story. I said rather emphatically to him, "We need your voice."

My request startled him into silence, but after a moment or two he replied, "I can't." Then he looked past me, out the window, as if he was reliving that time. "I can't," he repeated, this time in a halting voice. "I have kept that part of my life locked up. If I were to go back and relive it, I don't know what would happen to me."

I immediately regretted saying anything, thinking, what have I done? What if I had opened a door that should have remained shut? I quickly steered the conversation back to preplanning my funeral; we finished our business there, but I felt a lingering awkwardness. It is understandable that a Holocaust survivor might close the door to further self-examination and be afraid to confront unacknowledged emotions. Opening a closed door was a valid symbol. Closed doors, to me, represented all the fears and insecurities, and yes, hatreds, that haunted me. They are real, and they stand there, just beyond the doorway, patiently awaiting inspection.

Arthur used to call them "dwellers on the threshold." He viewed the "dwellers" (not to be confused with the term "the dweller on the threshold" used by Rudolf Steiner, Edward Bulwer Lytton, and others) as the unacknowledged resentments and hatreds that are actually unresolved challenges I need to face. In total, they are the most intimate aspects of the self; the deepest fears and hidden longings that the self doesn't want to recognize. Most people never meet their dwellers because the self does not confront them easily. Yet confrontation is a necessity. These dwellers will stand on the threshold, just beyond the border of recognition, until I confront them.

How do I do that? I never handled confrontation in my life very well. Up to this point, the "changes" in my life proved not to be changes at all, but rather life presenting the same challenge to me through different scenarios. I could only affect real change by opening that closed door.

Take, for example, my deep-seated fear of being lost. It was my first day of grade school. Mom needed to go to work and could drop me off, but she said I was going to get a ride home from Margaret's mom, a neighbor of ours on the same block. Unfortunately, the teacher split Margaret and me into two different classes, and I never did find her again to get that ride home. When school let out, I found a crossing guard and managed to explain, through my hysteria, my situation to her. Her husband worked for the fire department, and he escorted me home in his fire truck! My child mind thought my parents would be relieved to see me come home. I know I was relieved. However, they greeted me with laughter, as they thought a fire truck delivering their son home from his first day of school was funny. And I remembered that. Years later, the story of my being lost was good material for family stories at holiday time, and the laughter would start up again. I repressed many childhood experiences, but I remembered this one, most likely because they kept bringing it up to me.

I never traveled to strange places unless I had armed myself with a load of maps. If I had to go somewhere strange without a set of maps, I found a way not to go. I denied myself many opportunities to travel simply because my fear of being lost prevented me from exploring, which is such an indigenous characteristic for a child. In therapy, I realized how angry I was at my parents for laughing at me when I was scared out of my mind. I was angry because I felt abandoned. I was angry at feeling shamed for simply being lost. I discovered that when I am angry, it has less to do with a person or event than the fact that I feel afraid or unsafe in my surroundings.

Eventually, I spoke to my mother about it. I told her how I felt as a kid to come home as shaken as I was and be greeted with laughter instead of a "Welcome home, we're glad you're here and safe." My revelation shocked my mother. She hadn't thought of it that way, but she realized the effect it had had on me, and she apologized profusely. I accepted her apology, and we moved on. I never mentioned the incident again, and neither did she.

That memory was a dweller, and I think this sort of confrontation brings healing. Believing in past lives as I do, if I don't confront the dwellers, I know I will have to resolve them in another lifetime, for they remain a part of me. Whatever negative reactions I had to a life experience formed an energy that I created. I must reclaim it so that it dissolves and doesn't reside on the threshold anymore. I know there are other dwellers there, but my hope is to continue to acknowledge them so I can arrange for their passage.

Some years later, I was visiting friends in Tennessee. They had a beautiful house in a rural area some miles outside of Nashville. One day I decided to take a walk in the hills just behind their home. It was early fall; the weather was cool, and the sun was shining brightly. I kept walking; it was so beautiful, just looking and absorbing the surroundings…that, unfortunately, gradually transformed into trees towering over me. No house in sight. I froze when I realized what had happened, but I continued to breathe. Looking around would not help because each direction looked like the other three. How was I to get back to my friends? I stood still, very still, and tried to sense where I had started…and I walked in that direction…and the house appeared in sight.

A much larger dweller that I confronted was my mother's violation of my boundaries in childhood. Dad's abuse was recognizable; Mom's was not, and it took some serious reading, therapy, and time before I realized what had occurred. I did confront her one day when we were alone. I told her about ideas I learned in therapy about boundaries, and how, by confiding in me too personally, she had made me her "surrogate husband." I stated, as well as I could, that I felt violated by what had happened between us, and that I had never been able to fully be a child because I had grown up too quickly.

She listened carefully, and she understood. She apologized for putting me through the stress and conflict of her relationship with Dad. I remembered her lost tone and her frustration when she concluded with, "There wasn't a lot of information out there about alcoholism and my choices. I felt helpless. I wanted to help you since I saw how upset Dad made you. I didn't know what I was doing." That was enough for me; I accepted her apology. This conversation brought us closer as mother and son, adults, and friends.

William said he kept his Holocaust experiences locked up because he was afraid of what would happen to him if he examined them. Speaking for myself, what if I had kept my childhood abuse locked up and never examined it? What would have happened to me?

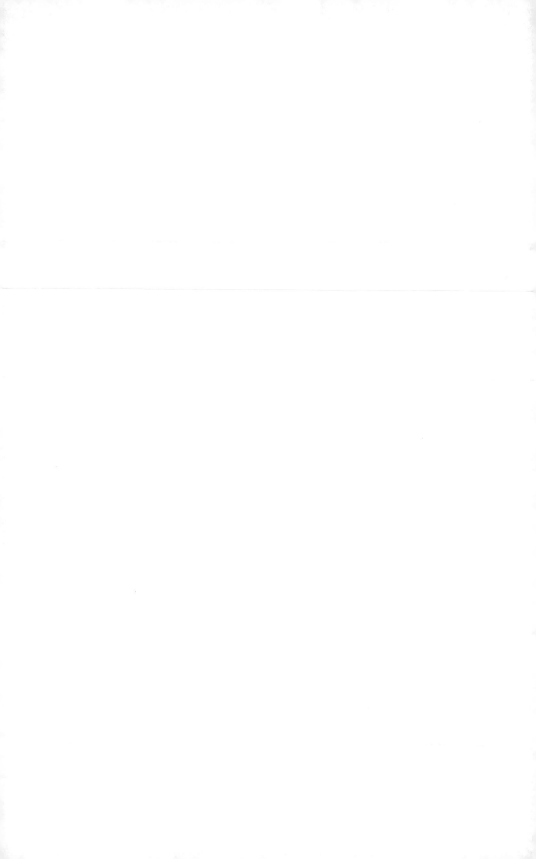

Judgment

⌒

Shiputim

The Proper Treatment of the Dead

No life is a waste.
Mitch Albom

⌒

The deceased was someone with AIDS and a prominent member of the LGBT community. The obituary in the paper was mean-spirited and cruel. The article seemed to be trying to show that the deceased person had no redeeming value. It felt as though the unflattering obituary was a way of settling the score over a long-standing feud.

My sadness over the obituary was that there was no compassion to balance the heavy dose of judgment. It is true that certain people are simply difficult, unsympathetic figures. Some of their actions are even horrifying, but we all have our lessons in life. Some learn those lessons, and their lives are a testimony to their growth. If others' lives do not provide similar testimonials, we cannot conclude they did not learn and grow. What if there were personal insights and realizations in their lives of which we have no firsthand knowledge? Maybe the soul *has* achieved a certain amount of success; maybe the internal changes necessary to produce growth have begun, but just not materialized in this physical life. No one has firsthand knowledge of others' internal struggles. That is between the soul and God. Even if the spark of goodness each person inherits from God never took flame, it was not a wasted life.

Having said that, I am also not aware of the obituary writer's own internal struggles with what might be a complicated relationship with the deceased. I did not know the deceased, nor did I know the author of the obituary. Yet even after admitting this, I cannot help but feel that this obituary was not complete, for it seems there is more than a physical body that needs to be buried, and that is judgment.

I feel that when I judge others I go to extremes and either idolize my heroes or demonize my enemies (or both). One person I idolized was Mom. I felt she could do no wrong, but I was mistaken. She enabled Dad to continue his drinking and placed her family at risk. Of course, I demonized Dad. If I had displayed an ounce of compassion toward him, I would have seen how liquor trapped him. I might have been more cognizant of his efforts to change. The realization that my parents were human didn't surface until much later. For the moment, I couldn't move past my own internal shame. I was stuck.

Judgment is such an indigenous quality in most religions, and it pours out furiously, even ferociously. If I place myself on a continuum of human behavior and am honest with myself, I will find I am somewhere in the middle, neither a *tzadik*, a holy person, nor a lost soul beyond the capacity to change. So is everyone else. In my opinion, this is where religion makes its mistakes. Truth will always break down when religion applies a dogmatic approach to its rules and regulations. Truth cannot thrive on the edges of extremism. Compassion quickly dies, breeding intolerance and fostering divisions. After compassion dies, wisdom becomes an elusive value, which people end up searching for in the holy books. We continue to search for it externally because we have forgotten we need to live our lives with compassion.

One of Abraham's first prayers was to ask God for compassion for the cities of Sodom and Gomorrah.[9] The cities of Sodom and Gomorrah no less! He was the embodiment of compassion. We cannot afford to be otherwise. If there is any judgment, it needs to be judgment with compassion. Judging compassionately follows a specific line of reasoning. There is always an explanation for another person's words or actions, but more often than not, I am not privy to it. Sometimes, if I am patient, I can discover those reasons simply by releasing my attachment to my judgment and letting life reveal itself. I can facilitate this discovery by pulling out of my self-absorbed personal world and becoming more aware of theirs.

It would take years, *years*, before I could view Dad and the life he created for himself and others with a compassionate approach. When I consider difficult unsympathetic figures, I would have to place Dad on that list. One evening Mom and I drove out for dinner. I was home from college, and we left without Dad, assuming he was drinking at the bar. I was ready to make a right turn into the restaurant when Mom screamed at me to stop. Dad was lying on the side of the road, facedown in the gravel, dressed in a suit. He was out cold.

He woke up briefly, wondering where he was, feebly protesting when we tried to carry him into the back seat of the car. He passed out again. Back home, Mom, in her frustration, gave up trying to undress him and just threw a blanket over him. He slept on the couch, in his suit, for almost twenty-four hours. I couldn't take any more and told Mom I was tired of rescuing him. All I ever did was take care of him. When was it going to be my turn? I told her he wasn't worth it and was making our lives miserable. I don't remember whether we ever ate at all, I was so upset.

I was hardly the "embodiment of compassion." If I really believed what I wrote about judging compassionately, I might have considered a very simple idea, and that was how did my father's parents raise him? That had a lot to do with how he raised me. That perception wouldn't come until later, but when it did, it provided a doorway to judging him compassionately. It does not deny the necessity to process the anger I had toward him that, unfortunately, I sometimes projected on others. When I was able to get in touch with and process this anger, compassion did shine through. Back then, the compassion I really needed to have for him (actually, for both of them) was beyond my capability.

The Jacket

Good judgment comes from experience, and experience comes from bad judgment.
Rita Mae Brown

I found it in the basement that afternoon and wondered how it got there. Then I remembered. Earlier that day, my partner, Michael, wanted to clean the upstairs closets and donate the clothing to the resale shop. I didn't realize he had moved the jacket. So I quickly grabbed it and brought it back upstairs, telling him rather emphatically, "This one stays." He didn't care for the jacket's styling, nor did he understand why I held onto it if I wasn't going to wear it. When we met years ago, I wore the jacket on a regular basis, but I didn't even look that good in it.

The jacket was vinyl, not leather. However, it had belonged to Steven. At the time Steven and I met, I had a genuine leather jacket that he admired. He suggested swapping jackets. Since I didn't see him as much as I would have liked, it felt good to wear something of his when he wasn't around.

It was just my size, but worn, and the sleeves were frayed. By the time the relationship was over, the jacket's condition was an accurate description of my relationship with him, worn and frayed. We ended up fighting a lot because each of our personalities wanted to control the relationship. Anger simmered just underneath the surface. I didn't realize how dangerous it was at the time.

But Steven was larger than life and that was the attraction. The magnetism of his personality was so strong I couldn't resist it, and I would always run back to him. He could talk to everyone freely and openly using large, magnanimous gestures. He was spontaneous. If he felt like singing, he would sing. His personality was the exact opposite of mine, which was too shy and self-conscious to lose myself in uninhibited self-expression.

Since Steven was HIV-positive, I tried to convince him to quit smoking and pay better attention to his diet and overall health. To be fair, part of the reason he was so sick was the AZT itself. At that time, it was common to prescribe a higher dosage of the drug, which kept him nauseated. He tried, but we both knew my efforts to encourage him in this area essentially amounted to making him over, which never works in a relationship. Even so, it was becoming harder to be with someone who didn't want to take care of himself. Resentments started. He resented me for trying to change him, and I resented him simply for not trying to do better. Eventually, we had one fight too many and I broke it off. He became progressively sicker and died of AIDS in 1994.

This jacket, which was a symbol of such a contentious relationship created a kneejerk emotional reaction within me at the prospect of losing it. Why, I asked myself, couldn't I let it go? It took a number of years, but I realized the jacket was a symbol for what Steven and I eventually did have in common: our HIV-positive status. After hearing the news I was positive, I remembered the immense sadness that surrounded me. I remembered sharing that news with my parents and seeing them cry.

There were support groups around, but the few I attended focused on preparing to die and getting one's affairs in order. I began to understand the frustration Steven must have felt when my energy levels dropped and it took all of my effort just to maintain my job. There was no energy left for much else. I managed to keep working in spite of the 101-degree fevers that consumed me over a period of three months. They would break periodically to give me some relief, yet keep returning.

At the time, I was seeing a doctor who prescribed only herbs, natural supplements, and mistletoe injections. My determination to follow this treatment modality ended on one Saturday morning when my energy was so low I had to crawl to the kitchen to make breakfast. By that time, my T cells (white blood cells) had plunged to 230 (normal range being 900–1400). My viral load skyrocketed to nearly 100,000 copies in the bloodstream. It was time to change doctors, and my new doctor promptly prescribed the infamous AZT that Steven took, with its nasty side effects. Nearly twenty-five years later, I am where Steven was years ago, although with the arrival of more effective drugs, my health is better. I suppose my soul told me I needed to be in his shoes (jacket?) to understand him. I think I do now.

I may not see the jacket on a daily basis now, but I am still not willing to give it up. However, I no longer puzzle over why it hangs in my closet. There's nothing more humbling than walking the path of someone you had judged. The more I have judged people; the more I have received judgments in other situations, sometimes eerily similar situations, a little later in life. It is a "transcendental echo," reminding me that the energy I used to judge others has returned to greet and remind me where I made a wrong turn. That truth is simple. As Jesus states in the Gospel of Luke chapter 6, verse 37–38, "Judge not, and you will not be judged…For the measure you give will be the measure you get back."[10]

Modern-Day Leprosy

The moment you criticize, you already have a barrier between yourself and them...
Jiddu Krishnamurti

*I*n the Torah, there is a portion called *Tazria-Metzora* that details the ritual procedures used when a person has skin afflictions. These skin afflictions were commonly called leprosy, or *tza-ra-at*, although some sages have disputed the idea that it was actually leprosy. There was a lot of fear and ignorance about this condition. The community separated the individual, who remained isolated until the individual was no longer unclean. The ultimate purpose of separation was a reintegration of the individual back into the community.[11]

Unfortunately, society today uses separation to isolate groups of people, cultures, or subcultures that it can't handle. As a result, the individual or group can feel separate from everyone else and "unclean." I was in this "unclean" state for years when I was growing up, wrestling with my sexuality, and feeling "separate from" everyone else. Living in this separated state, I unconsciously embraced all the erroneous notions that religion and society imposed, and could not accept the goodness that was mine from the very beginning. I could not function effectively within society because I was so attached to my separateness from it.

People who are HIV-positive are a good example. According to Malcolm Westfield, a master's-level psychologist with a practice in Chicago, Illinois, people who are HIV-positive deal with being "other than" and "separate from" everyone else. They carry this mantle and cannot drop it easily, even in places that should function to provide a secure place for the HIV-positive individual.[12] The inability to declare that I was HIV-positive and be comfortable with it certainly tended to isolate me from even the LGBT community. I felt marked.

Prejudicial reactions from outside groups might be understandable, yet what is it about our nature that we end up separating and dividing within our very own culture or subculture? Yes, I have experienced prejudice from the straight world, but there have been times when I have experienced worse from gay individuals and the gay community. A former supervisor, who was gay himself, harassed me because I was HIV-positive, telling me frankly that he "owned" me because no one else would hire me in my condition. When he refused to permit me to observe my religious holidays, I had to call my lawyer. The threat of litigation stopped the harassment, but the damage was done and I found another job fast.

Westfield, who is African American, provides a better example of the divisions within groups. He once told me, "If you are of black heritage but your skin color is not black enough, you are not acceptable in the eyes of the black community."[13] Along religious lines, I could use the same rationale: if you are not *this* or *that* denomination—and that denomination can be either Christian or Jewish or Muslim—you are not acceptable. Jews seem to define themselves by how they are different from other Jews in terms of denomination or ritual observance, as do the Muslims, as do fundamentalist Christians versus the more liberal Christian denominations. If you do not believe this way or that way, there is something wrong with you, and the implication is that you are not acceptable.

I wonder sometimes if society and religion have gone to such extremes that they define and separate us by our differences, losing sight of our humanness that we all have in common. Have we inadvertently created our own *tza-ra-at*, a leprosy, that, if left unchecked, can only continue to fester? Any experience that reinforces differences and makes us feel unacceptable is what really becomes unclean and infected in our lives.

There have been responses from some cultures to instill pride for being the people we are, e.g., Black Pride, Gay Pride. And while it is wonderful to exult in our differences, that diversity will only work in our favor when we take pride in our uniqueness at the same time that we emphasize the humanness that threads us all together. Taking pride in our differences lets us stand with dignity. Yet if we remain separated from each other…aren't we still standing on the sidelines, alone?

I think the emphasis has to start on the goodness and value of each individual. Society's approach to the individual's place in community has become selective rather than inclusive, and as a result does not embrace those values. I think that we can facilitate inclusiveness and ultimately, healing, through education. Programs that cut across lines of religion, sexual orientation, and gender are a start. With continued emphasis on what unites us, and on listening to and affirming each other, we can begin to see that what we think are lines of separation are really spokes stemming from the same wheel, the wheel of an integrated community.

Time is important. It takes time for consciousness to grow until a definite "tipping point" occurs. Then that collective consciousness will lurch forward and materialize. Take, for example, the growing support for equal marriage rights. This push did not happen overnight. It was a long effort, with widespread public support developing over a number of years. Widespread support for equal marriage rights and the changes in law materialized with greater intensity in 2013.

As I mentioned in the first paragraph of this chapter, there was once a lot of fear and ignorance about leprosy. Fear is the root of all irrational judgment. Fear runs out of control in our culture, like a roller coaster unable to stop. It affects our ability to form wise judgments. Fear is our leprosy.

Grief

~

Avel

Walking with a Limp

But I must take another journey; we must meet with other names…
Jeannette Obstoj / The Fixx / Secret Separation

❧

In 1987, Arthur died of a sudden heart attack. I felt the need to seek help in dealing with my loss. My grief counselor told me, in our first session together, that it would help me to write. "Write, write, and continue to write," she said. I had previously written a daily journal, but my writing was sporadic at best. Now I wrote with more dedication. I wrote down everything, dreams, daily events, reflections, joys, and sorrows. Obviously, my writing reflected mostly sorrows during that time because I was one big emotional mess. Nevertheless, there were some important insights that I was able to glean from the text. In hindsight, all of the writing proved to be cathartic. These discoveries led to closure, for I later recognized the classic signs of the grieving process (anger, bargaining, depression, denial, and acceptance) within the pages of the journal. I am quoting several passages to show my reflections along that path, along with my comments.

Journal entry January 26, 1987

Last night, Arthur appeared to me in a very short and simple dream. "It's time for me to go," he said. I replied "okay" and that was that. When I met him on the corner of Clark and Belmont the next day and told him about it, he smiled, but didn't comment. Ten days later, he was dead from a heart attack on the Chicago CTA L platform.

Journal entry Feb 5, 1987

Dreamt Arthur told me "Advantage is had from that which is there. Opportunity arises from that which is not.'[14] I am giving you the opportunity to be independent. Take advantage of it." I was familiar with the passage about advantage and opportunity because that was his favorite passage from the Tao Te Ching,[vii] but independence was not a familiar word for me, and to be honest, it was a scary one.

I did not care for the sound of it at the time. His death was to be an advantage? At the time, I was too emotional to have a detached perspective about it. It would take time before I could see how prophetic his words were.

Journal entry Feb 7, 1987

Dreamt Arthur was in the living room of the new house, which he bought just three months ago. I was in the den. He asked me to take the information I would find in his files and write them into my own ledger. When I was through writing a line in my file, I crossed out the corresponding line in his file. When I transferred all the information over to my files, he told me to destroy his files and create my own. I woke up remembering his words, "This is what I leave you. I have done all I could. Forget my mistakes and work with what I have given you."

---

vii The *Tao Te Ching* is the fundamental text of Taoism.

I learned that Arthur merely provided the foundation for me. I needed to create something that was uniquely my own rather than just parrot his teachings. What was more important was what did I think? What was on my mind? I needed to find my own divine brilliance. When I did that, I would find the independence to which he was referring. That didn't happen until my conversion to Judaism seven years later.

Journal entry April 10, 1987

I decided to clean up around the house to keep busy. I wondered if I could use anything in the basement. Finding nothing that would be of help to me, I turned to go, when I noticed his clothes. They were in boxes in the enclosed back porch waiting for a pick-up from some friends. I honestly never paid attention to them before this because his mother had bundled all his clothes up.

I saw his winter coat on top of the pile, the one with the red lining, the one he was wearing when he died, and picked it up. I was holding onto his coat tightly, clutching it, as if doing so would bring him back to me, but it didn't work. I only started crying again. I started crying for him, telling myself "this is ridiculous." No matter how much I scolded myself for crying, I continued to cry and I think I cried as much for the shock of losing him suddenly as I cried for him.

Yet I am mad at him for leaving. I ended up cussing him out; using every four-letter word I could think of. I even surprised myself by throwing a few pots at the walls. I felt terrible for hating him. I really did hate him.

I had been doing a lot of crying. I found myself riding emotional waves that would rise up at the most inopportune times in public (I used one washroom with a loud fan at work so that no one could hear my sobbing, which would often spontaneously erupt). I would catch myself travelling between moments of illusion ("this is just a dream"), to lucidity ("I know he's gone"), to sheer emotional madness (crying at the slightest memory and continuing to cry until I didn't know where the tears were coming from anymore). I felt out of control.

I wondered, rather egotistically, whether he grieved for his separation from me. That was an interesting concept. It made sense to me because I wanted him to be missing me. I think the departed do grieve in a sense, although it is probably a different form of grieving, since they are in a nonphysical dimension. Once I am free from the physical body, my vision will expand, and I will understand more about the life I have lived. I also believe I will have to undergo a self-examination, which will include all the emotional attachments I had to the individuals I loved or feared. The bottom line here is I cannot believe that I am the only one grieving, just because death has forced a disconnection from Arthur's and my interaction on the physical level.

Journal entry October 10, 1987

I remember all the long talks about religion, philosophy, and methodologies such as Astrology[viii] and Tarot.[ix] Sometimes we would just sit in the living room for three or four hours, talking. At other times, we would take walks in the park or around town and discuss these matters. It was a natural thing for us to do and became part of our routine.

---

viii The study of the movement and position of planetary and related celestial bodies to predict human behavior and events. These predictions are considered to be influential in nature and not necessarily fated.

ix A pack of playing cards used in the fifteenth century that contained symbolism used for divination by mystics and occultists.

We talked a lot about reincarnation.[x] *Both of us knew our past lives well. We discovered them together through a series of past-life regressions conducted by professional hypnotists, trained in the art of guiding an individual to visit the past lives that might be affecting their current one. As we continued to study and meditate on these concepts, we made our own personal discoveries.*

One of those lifetimes was in France where he was a cardinal and I was a nun. He would visit me and together we would walk the gardens. We realized then where our walking routine originated. Both of us loved our solitude in that life. I died of a heart attack back then. In this lifetime, Arthur died of the heart attack. Perhaps we needed to swap experiences so we knew what it felt like to experience a loss by sudden death?

A rather poignant event occurred in 2009 when doctors diagnosed me with cardiovascular issues. I found that very interesting, and probably very appropriate, in light of the above history. It demonstrated to me how certain patterns repeated themselves over several lifetimes and were not yet ready to dissolve. I saw this concept illustrated effectively in the 2012 movie *Cloud Atlas*, with Tom Hanks.

We experienced other lifetimes together in Greece and Israel where he again functioned as a mentor to me. However, the lifetime with the most influence on this current physical one was the one in France with our love for solitude and our walking routine.

---

x   Latin, "to enter the flesh again." The transmigration of souls. The belief that this physical life is not the only one a soul experiences. Multiple lifetimes is a common belief in Eastern religions as well as in Spiritualism. It is a tenet associated with Kaballah, a mystical discipline of Judaism, and to a certain extent, in the more obscure, mystical aspects of Christianity as well.

It also explains why I loved my life in the seminary; the daily routine provided a large amount of time for privacy. What I learned is that my so-called "past" existences are not separate from each other, or from my current life for that matter. I remembered this idea later when analyzing my relationship with my mother. It partially explained the violation of boundaries inflicted upon me.

Journal entry June 30, 1990

I dreamt of Arthur. He was wearing a white shirt and black pants. He showed me a jewel embedded in a plate of glass, which turned out to be a watch. He pointed to it and said, "See? It's still ticking." That was one of the many things I loved about him; he found delight in the simplest of things.

I felt he was trying to say that time itself is a jewel, even without him. It was time to move on. I knew I had spent years crying over him, but he was warning me not to "die to time," remaining frozen in a cycle of grief that I wouldn't be able to break. All I needed to do was the best that I could do. As he told me in one of my earliest dreams, "Never underestimate yourself. Do that for me."

I kissed him on the cheek and said, "I love you." He looked at me; half smiled, and replied, "I love you, too." Then he disappeared.

Arthur never told me he loved me when he was physically here (he said "likewise," but he could never say the exact words). In the dream, the words fell off his tongue so easily. This was evidence of progress on his part in expressing his emotions. Even better than that, this dream revealed to me that I was on the mend. I would be okay.

From that point on, I stopped dreaming of him. Little memories, happy memories of our life together began to surface. I used to kid him about the twenty-two pairs of sunglasses (!) that he left in rooms around the house. "Why do you keep so many?" I once asked him. "In case I run out," was his answer. That recollection provided a good laugh. He had such a droll sense of humor. He was a beautiful soul and I was blessed to have had him in my life. To this day, I miss the Teacher-student relationship we had. He has taken the correct place as a part of my life, an important part to be sure, but one that does not eclipse my living in the here and now.

There were times when I felt I would never get over his death, but continuing to tell myself that only limited my ability to heal. I did get over it; I just will never the same. I have never reached a space where I didn't miss him, and that's okay. Frankly, there are still times I cry in solitude, longing for his presence. An appropriate sentiment for how I feel is in the movie *The Upside of Anger.* Kevin Costner tells a grieving Joan Allen that you never get over the loss of a loved one. "It heals. It just heals funny. You more or less learn to walk with a limp."[15] And I do.

Guilt

Ashma

Guilty of Not Being Good Enough

Guilt is perhaps the most painful companion of death.
Coco Chanel

After I received the news of Arthur's death, one of the first people I called was Liz, a former work acquaintance of his. When she heard the news, she didn't say anything for a few seconds. Then she slowly responded, "Well, you know we were supposed to have dinner tonight. But if he didn't want to go, all he had to do was call and cancel!" An attempt at humor did not comfort her. She went home and cried for the rest of the day. I went home and cried for five years.

During those years, I carried a heavy feeling that I later identified as my guilt. I searched a long time and unsuccessfully tried to discover why I felt so guilty. A good friend told me about a meditation process where one could obtain insight by asking for forgiveness from your loved one. I decided to try it.

I began by searching the history of our lives together and enumerating my offenses. Long pauses separated each incident I recalled, probably because of the strangeness involved in the exercise, but I also think it was just difficult to confront myself. "Forgive me… forgive me…forgive me…" As soon as I named each incident, I felt like it was no longer submerged and trapped.

A growing list of events about which I felt guilty mentally stood in line, waiting for expression. There were no pauses now, and the rhythm of my chanting felt like the *Al Cheit*[xi] I recited on Yom Kippur.[xii] I continued, "…Forgive me for this transgression… Forgive me for that omission, etc…" Then, finally, a thought erupted that stopped me dead in my tracks: "Forgive me for not being a good enough friend." I stopped and absorbed what I had just said. That was it. That was the emotional root of my guilt. A continued search revealed nothing more, and I felt myself sink into a place of silence and serenity.

Further examination of our life together revealed many circumstances where I was there for him and showed my love for him. Yet I still felt I wasn't good enough. I felt our relationship should have been measure for measure. I failed to understand that the relationship between two souls doesn't always function in this manner.

A friend wrote to me that after a loved one dies, the natural impulse is to think we haven't done enough. Whatever this "enough" is, it is

---

xi A confession of community sins recited numerous times on Yom Kippur.

xii Literally "Day of Atonement," the holiest day of the year for those of the Jewish faith. The day is marked by prayer services (there are five throughout the day), public confession of sin, private prayer, and fasting.

a mythical concept. It is nonexistent. If we were to do this mythical "enough," we would deprive everyone else of our time, our energy, and our love. When guilt rushes in, we saddle ourselves with not having done "enough."

After my mother's death, I found myself confronting guilt all over again. One night I dreamt of waiting to take the train. An announcement blared over the loudspeaker announcing its arrival. I entered a walkway and saw Mom below. She walked toward me, looking like she did at age twenty or twenty-five. She walked over all these platforms and when she found me, exclaimed joyfully, "I've been trying so hard to reach you." I know I talked at length with her, but I woke up with the remembrance of asking her only one question: "Was I a good enough son?" There it was again, same song, second verse.

How did my parents' deaths change my understanding of myself? I thought I was insufficient or not good enough without them. I couldn't do enough for Mom, yet failed to realize what I did for her was more than enough. Most things I did for Dad did not meet with his approval. There was always something I could have done better. Maybe he wanted me to improve myself, but I didn't come out of childhood with that feeling. The few times I earned Dad's approval from a project I completed around the house, such as painting a room, I mentally soared into heaven. I was that happy. It was such a change of pace from the criticism.

The feeling of not being good enough has certainly led to my perfectionism in life, which, even if I did not express it verbally, haunted me in the form of mental judgments that lingered within my head and ultimately made me less forgiving toward others and myself. Things had to be perfect so I wouldn't receive any criticism. As perfect as I wanted to be, I needed to realize it was okay for me not to be perfect because that was part of being human. This is one of my life's major lessons. Relax. Lighten up. I am still working on this.

It's tempting to dismiss these comments as self-indulgent rambling about the dead and departed that have no relevance to anyone other than me. I know we all have our stories. There is a lot of knowledge in any story, but without a confrontation with the self, the knowledge in those stories is only dead food. Just as the body absorbs the nutrients in food, my soul needed to absorb the lessons created when my loved ones died.

The drama within my stories will only perpetuate itself until I make a serious effort at confronting my feelings. If I don't do that, I seal the doors to my self-discovery and mark them "self-imprisonment." The passage of time will only leave me dancing on the perimeter of my pain and guilt, never fully embracing it, never fully confronting it. I need to wrestle with it so a new dialogue can emerge within the self, a dialogue that can lead to healing.

Realization

Hakara

Peeling the Onion

The unexamined life is not worth living.
Socrates

⌒

The Gospel of Matthew chapter 5, verse 16 states, "In the same way, let your Light shine before others, so that they may see your good works..."[16] Kabbalists[xiii] refer to Light, too. One of their main principles is that we are here to share our Light with others. It is so difficult to share my Light with others if I don't really know how I help or hinder the divine brilliance that is mine. That requires self-examination. The process is similar to peeling an onion. Each layer of the onion represents some belief I have embraced or behavior I have adopted to protect myself from being hurt. They are mostly my fears, which find expression through anger and judgment.

---

xiii A student or teacher of Kabbalah, the mystical branch of Judaism.

Peeling the layers carries the risk of tears, just as with peeling an onion. Correspondingly, how much I peel when I confront myself depends on my willingness to be vulnerable with myself. If I can remain in that space of being vulnerable I can continue to ask questions until I find further insight. It is a method to increase awareness and is similar to the process I used to analyze my guilt after Arthur's death. In this case, rather than making statements, I am asking questions.

Growing up, I learned never to question anything. Too many questions, or the wrong questions, generated a dismissive gesture, a stern rebuke, or even a slap from Dad. I very quickly learned to shut up and stop questioning. As I grew older, the more I neglected my self-examination, the more the portions of my unexamined self remained anchored to the past, and perpetuated my current issues. I needed to start by acknowledging what is currently operating in my life; I needed to acknowledge what *is* before I could move into what can be.

I prepared a list of questions, segmented into categories for simplicity's sake, but there really is no separation between them when I view the categories as a comprehensive whole. I wrote these questions with myself in mind. Please understand that I have considered the following statements acceptable for me. I do not say them to make blanket statements for others experiencing the same life event(s). Perhaps there is some relevancy for others, perhaps not. That is okay. This is my self-examination.

The Physical World

Do I make the effort to take care of my body and any health concerns? Do I refuse to seek help because I am too afraid or proud to admit I need help? Are my needs for water, food, and rest ignored? Do I drink or eat too much? What am I saying about my self-worth when I overindulge or neglect myself to this extent?

Can I look past my physical ailments to see what my soul is trying to express? Many metaphysical teachers and authors, most notably Louise Hay, have said that if we listen to our bodies, we will know the mental work we need to perform to make the necessary corrections.[17] Physical events that affect my body function as symbols, reflecting beliefs about myself. String the symbols together and they tell a story about where my consciousness is now. A correspondence exists between a physical ailment and an erroneous belief, which is the original source of the malady. With this in mind, I began to look at my childhood ailments in the light of my experiences.

My epilepsy: I learned to be afraid to express my emotions. I was so angry with Dad when I was young, but he would slap me when I expressed that anger. Both anger and epilepsy had a common thread, and that was a loss of control. It seems reasonable to assert that my epilepsy was an expression of how I felt within the home. The seizures were my soul's method of expressing the helplessness and lack of validation I felt as a child.

My hearing: I lost nearly 90 percent of it at age ten. I shut myself down from the outside world and didn't want to "hear" all the fights and arguments going on around me. No one was listening to me anyway, so correspondingly I expressed the belief, physically, that I wasn't going to hear what anyone had to say.

My HIV status: I think back to my friend Steven, whom I mentioned in "The Jacket." I can see that while it may have been true that I needed to experience what he was going through, my HIV status and subsequent poor health was also a consequence of how poorly I thought of myself. I felt I was unlovable for many years and that I did not deserve to be here. If I felt this way, then what "better" illness could there be to reflect my mental state of being than a disease that robbed me of the ability to function on this earth?

My recent developments with heart problems, nerve, and bone issues follow along the lines of the same thinking. I had become so critical and judgmental of others (when people got on my nerves) that my ability to be compassionate (heart health) withered. I often felt unsupported by others (poor bone density).

The Emotional World

What is the status of my emotional response to life? Am I compassionate to those I meet even if I don't understand them? Do I allow my emotions to create connections to other people? Have I taken things too personally and created a distance from others by wrapping myself in a metaphorical blanket of thorns, the pain of which only reminds me of old resentments and hurts? Sadly, I mastered this one as I bounced from one emotional crisis to another.

The Mental World

What is the status of my mental life? Do I develop my mind to facilitate its growth by learning something new? Refusing to listen to new ideas can only lead to arrogance. Is my vision one that includes all viewpoints or is my thinking in black and white? Am I so critical that every thought is a judgment?

The Exterior World

How reactive am I to my experiences? When I react to people or situations, positively or negatively, it is because there is some resonance of those qualities within myself. Whatever turns me on or off about a person or event is a clue to what I need to examine in myself. The most startling revelation here was discovering my annoyance with people who are indecisive. Yet, I am indecisive by nature. Life is a mirror.

Are appropriate boundaries in place between others and myself to establish a healthy definition of who I am? Do I feel so overwhelmed that I have to create boundaries by building walls of anger in order to guard myself from people?

Do I try to rescue people who cross my path? There is a difference between helping someone and saving someone. As much as I wanted to help certain people, I had to learn to back off, not out of a lack of empathy, but in order to protect myself.

I remember the number of people I dated after college. I discovered a pattern among them—they all had drinking problems! I would try to "help" them, arrogantly thinking that because of my background with my father, I was qualified to do so. One fellow defiantly snapped at me, "I'm not your father. I can hold my liquor!" Of course, he couldn't. I lost myself trying to save them, but I finally learned to walk away. I learned I could help people as long as I didn't enable them.

The Interior World

Do I accept the unique qualities about myself? For years, I fought my introverted nature. Thinking there was something wrong with me, I tried desperately to fit in with groups or clubs, with sad or even disastrous results. I felt I was wearing someone else's clothing. It was another instance of feeling different from everyone else and, as a result, separate from them.

I jealously coveted my privacy and returned to it when I pushed myself to be "out there" in the social crowd. Over time, I learned it was not only okay to be who I am; there was value in it, great value. I learned how to say, "This is who I am." The world needs introverts as much as it does extroverts. I revel in my introverted nature, and not surprisingly, I function more effectively in social situations because I have learned how to be true to myself. My relationship with my partner thrives as it does because Michael respects my need to be alone at times.

The Sexual World

Do I joyously accept my sexuality? Can I view it as a gift? Can I fully embrace that no part of me is evil or cursed? For too many years, I absorbed the erroneous teaching that I needed to change my nature, and that, as my seminary confessor told me, God had given me a cross to bear. This approach was the basis for the "less than" feeling I mentioned in "Modern-Day Leprosy."

The Spiritual World

What is the status of my spiritual life? Am I aware of God as I live my daily life? Or is God a Presence I just visit in temple? In my darkest times, have I forgotten God and constructed a spiritual tower of isolation, a tower in which I live, a place where God and others can't enter because I have locked the door? Do I feel part of God or separate from Him?

I like the following Hasidic[xiv] story. It emphasizes the need to review the self periodically so we can reveal the light of our own divine brilliance in this world.

"Where are you running to?" asked the Talmud[xv] professor of a young Yeshiva[xvi] student hurrying by.

"I'm rushing home to look over the machzor[xvii] before I have to lead services," the student replied, trying to catch his breath.

"The prayer book hasn't changed since last year," said the old sage. But perhaps you have. Go home and look over yourself."[18]

---

xiv "To be pious or kind." Hasidism is a mystical Jewish movement founded in the eighteenth century by the Baal Shem Tov (literally, Master of the Good Name).

xv The Talmud is a book of oral law or rabbinic rulings on theology, ethics, customs, philosophy, etc. Sometimes called the Oral Torah, it is a central text of Judaism, second only to the Torah. There are two versions. The Palestinian Talmud originated in 375 BCE. The Babylonian Talmud was from 500 BCE.

xvi One who attends a Jewish educational institution focused on the study of Torah and Talmud.

xvii Prayer book used in the High Holy Day services. The weekly prayer book is called a siddur. The machzor is a stylized siddur used for special occasions.

The Prayer Connection

The Greatest Prayer is Patience.
Hindu Prince Gautama Siddharta

Rabbi Douglas Goldhamer from Congregation Bene Shalom, a synagogue for the deaf and hearing in Skokie, Illinois, told me the reason religion didn't work for most people was that they didn't maintain a consistency in their devotion to or communication with God. People only thought of God on the Sabbath, the High Holidays,[xviii] or when they experienced a crisis in their lives. Then they would remember God and say extra prayers or run to put money in the *pushke*.[xix] God answered their prayers and spoke

---

xviii Also known as the Days of Awe, the High Holidays are a ten-day period of repentance and self-reflection. The Ten Days of Repentance, as they are also called, begin with Rosh HaShanah and end with Yom Kippur.

xix Yiddish for "charity box." A can or container kept in the home for the collection of charity to be disbursed later.

to them, but the relationship they had with God was connected with only a thin string, to use an analogy, and that connection was too weak for anyone to hear God's answer. A consistent effort to maintain our relationship with God is important, rather than a grand declaration made at isolated times on religious holidays.[19]

That was my problem. All my life I had prayed to God only when I wanted something, and in my early twenties I concluded that just like me, God had a severe hearing problem because He didn't answer my prayers. It was natural for me to doubt He existed at all.

However, I eventually did understand that when I prayed for something from God, I often didn't obtain what I prayed for directly, but instead received the opportunities to develop what I needed. During a particularly trying time, when I had asked for patience, I ended up only finding myself in more life situations in which I needed to develop patience. How frustrating it was to discover I would not receive patience on a silver platter. No, it was through my efforts, both my failed and my successful efforts, that patience could become a part of me. The experience of being patient with life events could become so woven into the fabric of my soul that I could realize it, I could make it mine. Then there could be no way for the threads to unravel, so in effect, I would never lose it.

To pray, "Help me, God" really means help me to reach the Divinity within myself to know God is never separate from me. It is an ongoing process. In His own way, God had answered my prayers. I just didn't see it at the time. I still confront life situations when I need patience, evidence that this is an ongoing lesson. The interesting part is that these occurrences are less frequent, and my impatience when they occur is much less severe in intensity. I am learning.

The Prayer of Gratitude

If you see no reason for giving thanks, the fault lies in yourself.
Tecumseh

⟶

I define gratitude as the acknowledgement I give to God for the blessings in my life. Too often, when God answered my prayers, I neglected to return to Him to acknowledge His answers. Returning to Him to acknowledge the blessings given is the final piece in this prayer cycle that began with "The Prayer Connection."

Growing up, I thought there was nothing to be grateful for because I focused on everything I didn't have, the most obvious thing being health. It was hard to be grateful to God when I was in the midst of pain, trying to shake off some illness. However, as I continued to search, I found there was much for which I could be thankful, even in the middle of a crisis. I began by comparing myself with other people who were more disadvantaged or had worse challenges. While I felt grateful I didn't have their problems, it wasn't really the right approach to use, and ultimately, it didn't make me feel any better. In fact, it reminded me of Luke chapter 18, verse 9–13, where the Pharisee and the Publican are praying in temple. The Pharisee thanked God that He didn't make him like the Publican.[20] That's what my prayers of gratitude felt like. They felt wrong to me. As time passed, I learned to be grateful for my life because it was my life, and not because I compared it with anyone else's.

When I look back, the very first tangible thing I remembered appreciating was a place to live after leaving my parents' home so abruptly. It was a simple $60-per-month room in a boarding house. The room had holes in the ceiling (which leaked when it rained), and a closet with stairs that led to the basement (and neither the upstairs or downstairs door could be locked). The bathroom was a communal one with a broken mirror and a rusty shower stall. My mother was horrified that I left her house for this "rat hole," as she put it. Yet, for the first time in years, I slept through the night in my own bed. It didn't matter what condition the room was in; it was mine, it was home, and I remembered loving it for the peace it gave me. (I realized much later how my new physical environment, cracked mirror and all, was an appropriate external picture for how damaged I felt internally.) At that moment, it was perfect, and I was grateful I had it.

Something else I could be grateful for was food. While I was living in that room and years later, studying in Virginia, supporting myself meant just being able to afford the rent and utilities and food. Many times the food was far simpler fare than I wanted to eat; sometimes it was only one meal a day, usually peanut butter and crackers, at least until the next paycheck arrived. I do remember the sense of gratitude I had for even that.

There were other things I learned to acknowledge as well, intangible things: freedom to worship, friendships, children, grandchildren. The more I used my mind to think about my life and the people in it, the more blessings I discovered. The list grew. By being mentally receptive to all the goodness that was around me, I allowed gratitude to open the door for continued sustenance. Over time, gratitude eventually became a state of being rather than a prayer to perform.

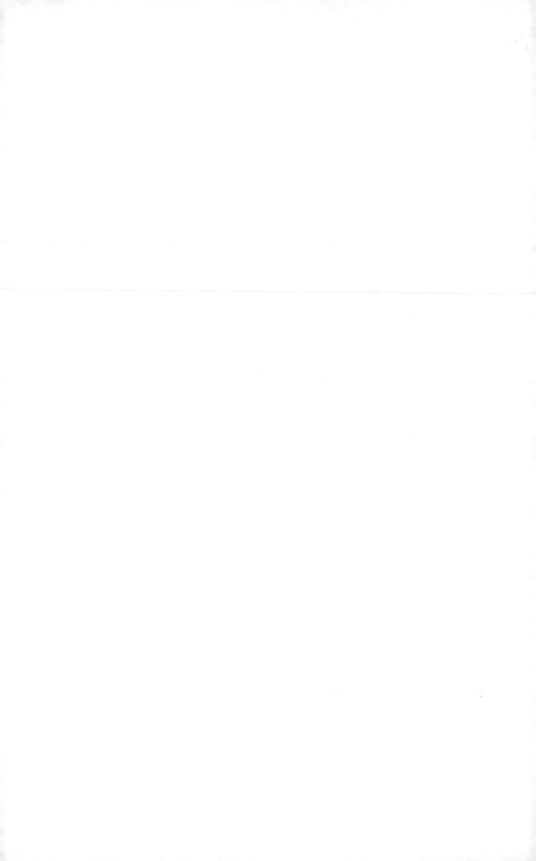

Giving Back

For it is in giving that we receive.
St. Francis of Assisi

⁓

I was living in that boarding house when I met Arthur. He paid for the entertainment expenses, even if it was the simplest of dining options, such as cheap take-out. Sensing my discomfort at always being on the receiving end, he spoke rather directly and said, "Sometimes it is necessary to receive when another must give. All have the need to give and receive. When the time is right, you will find the circumstances by which you can pay me back. You'll know."

He died a number of years later, and I never did find those circumstances. After his death, walking through downtown Chicago, I noticed that every homeless person seemed to know where I was and would ask for money. I would give them a small donation, but then I would turn a corner and another one would approach me. I dismissed it as a sign of the hard economic times in which we were living. I just couldn't give to everyone, and I was only one person.

One day I gave money to a homeless couple, a bit more than I usually donated. Rather than view the couple as taking advantage of me, as a friend implied, I concluded the lesson I needed to learn was not to be less gullible, but to give back because my life was a little bit better financially. The hungry and the homeless stood as a living model of my need to give more. It was as if the Universe was saying, "Time to give back." That assessment certainly felt true for me.

I discovered organizations that assisted the hungry, such as Food for the Poor, and gave what money I could. I felt my money could do more good there, and established a habit of writing checks every month. Then an interesting event occurred. Walking down the street, no one approached me for donations. It was as if either they didn't see me, or I didn't cross their paths, yet I hadn't changed my walking route. Once I gave back, there was no need for their presence and the message they had come to give me. My consciousness must have changed.

I can learn from everyone who crosses my path in life. They model right in front of me what I should be learning. When I reviewed my life in this context, with all of the figures who had played a positive and negative part in it, I know I chose these people to teach me. Whether I learned the lesson or not, I think I chose well.

When I reflected on this experience, Arthur's words came back to me: "When the time is right, you will find the circumstances by which you can pay me back. You'll know." I found those circumstances, but it wasn't Arthur who needed repayment.

Receiving Graciously

You aren't alive if you aren't in need.
Henry Cloud

I think religious practice is easier for individuals with a healthy sense of self-esteem. It was hard to adopt the Christian or Jewish attitude about humility and sacrifice when my self-worth was so beaten up to begin with. Buddhism, in particular, with its denial of the ego, is particularly challenging. Applying the religious concept of thinking of others before the self antagonizes the unmet buried needs of a child. When I tried to assert my needs, I also had to deal with the guilt that surfaced over that assertion, complicating the issue. I had a difficult time determining what was normal. It does not help if you never received the support and affirmation of your own needs.

Under the guise of independence, I refused to turn to anyone for my needs, figuring I could handle it myself. I know I was making it harder on myself, but I hadn't learned to accept the kindness and generosity that others were willing to give to me. I couldn't accept it because it would make me vulnerable, and I didn't want to be in that space. I didn't know how to receive very well because I viewed receiving as not normal, something I didn't deserve to accept.

What changed my perception was the surgery I required in 2009. The doctors called it minor surgery since it was only a two-day stay in the hospital, but I felt it was major. The recuperation that followed turned out to be the bigger challenge. The procedures (an angioplasty with three stents, followed by a coronary atherectomy, a clearing of the carotid artery) and the cardiac rehab that followed weren't as important to me as what I learned about myself in the process of healing afterward.

As I stated before, my memories of my childhood were scarce, since I had repressed most of them due to my abuse. Shortly after the surgery, from out of the depths of that repression, I recalled an incident. (Did the clearance of a 70 percent blocked artery stimulate the release of that memory? Since the memory surfaced around the same time, it was, at the very least, an interesting correspondence.) My memory was of when I developed my hearing loss, which was about the third major illness to occur in my childhood. I remembered my dad telling Mom, "He's not worth it." I heard them during one of their usual arguments. This time the argument was over a new treatment for my ears that required weekly visits to the doctor and was rather expensive.

Now, he could have said, "*It's* not worth it," but ultimately, it didn't matter which word he used. I heard his refusal to help me from the standpoint of a little boy, concluding in my child mind, "I'm not good enough." The remembrance of that statement, along with the intensity of the argument and the impact of the words, hit me. My parents were arguing over my value. This event occurred shortly after Christmas, the one Christmas when Dad chose not to give me or my younger brother any gifts. There was nothing for us under the tree. It was easy for me to conclude that I must have been a bad boy and didn't deserve to receive any gifts, and being a bad boy, I didn't deserve to have my needs met. My behavior as an adult started to make sense.

During and after the angioplasty and carotid surgery, I would be dependent on others for help. An important lesson I needed to learn was to receive graciously the caring that family and friends gave me. Even more significant was the care that Michael gave me because it represented what my father was incapable of giving to me when I was young.

Since depression was a side effect of the surgery, Michael let me be without criticism. I could act crazy, I could cry, I could be emotionally upset, and he did not react. There was no judgment. He was simply there for me. My job now was to let him give so I could receive. To resist his efforts now would be to continue to tell myself that I was simply "not worth it." I let him cook the meals. I even let him paint his bathroom, which I had been doing shortly before the surgery (now letting that go was painful, sorry to say, since I am much more thorough when it comes to house-hold jobs). I felt I was starting to come full circle toward healing the past because I had started to transform an energy pattern that needed correction. I was learning to receive without guilt.

I still fought Michael when he wanted to give. He assured me that he would cover any medical bills, and I reverted to my habit of refusing. No, I will take care of it, I told him, even if I have to pay it over time on my credit card. That led to a heated discussion. Finally, I gave in, and after a few moments of silence, I told him, "I know I am a complicated man. I am grateful that you love me so much." He replied, "We're all complicated, Yehuda. That's what makes us so loveable. There's no value in simplicity."

Now, I know correction itself is not as simple as this little discovery, but it's a start. Realization must occur first, and now that this realization was mine, what I needed to do was perform the mental work to extricate myself from the pain of my erroneous beliefs, step into my goodness, and receive graciously, because I am worthy and I deserve it.

Return

Chazara

True Religion

⟨⟩

*L*ast spring, a former friend sent us a "Dear John" letter in which he dissolved our friendship. Part of the letter read as follows, "...and I think it is a shame that Yehuda ever converted to Judaism when it should have been the other way around. Michael should have converted to Christianity. I don't know what you believe anymore, but it's obvious you're not going to heaven, which is where I'm going."

Thinking about who had access rights to heaven gave way to a memory from fourth grade. Back then, the nuns told us to pray for the Jews. Pray, they said, because the Jews will not go to heaven unless they convert, for we, as Catholics, had the True Religion. A few years later, when a visiting priest delivered a presentation on seminary life, a light went on in my twelve-year-old brain. I would become a priest so I could convert the Jews. I told myself it would be easy since I had the True Religion. How would the Jews not be able to see that?

Shortly after the receipt of our friend's letter, we were shopping at Nordstrom for a shirt when a special display of men's cologne caught my attention. I did a double take when I saw the name of the cologne in bold letters: True Religion. I thought of asking God if He was trying to tell me something, or if He was just being sarcastic. I decided not to risk it. The synchronicity of the two events was too unnerving.

When I converted, I learned about the different denominations and movements within Judaism, and was grateful for the variety of expression. The shock was that these denominations seemed to be monitoring one another's demonstration of the rites and rituals, when they could have been looking inward for their own demonstration, or lack of it. I found myself judging them…for judging me.

Rabbi Alan Lew, in *One God Clapping—the Spiritual Path of a Zen*[xx] *Rabbi*, states, "In all the major religions today, there are battles being fought between the dogmatists, who are old, tired, and dull, encased in their forms, and those advocating renewal and seeking to enliven the tradition at all costs, even to the point of embracing the latest spiritualist fads and leaving tradition in the dust altogether. Both sides lack what the other has. Those who reject tradition suffer because they have no standard outside themselves, and those who see God's word as frozen end up worshipping a dead God."[21]

---

xx Zen, simply defined, is a sect of Buddhism that emphasizes using total focus of the mind and body and dropping self-created illusions.

Mike and I had just moved into our townhouse in the middle of summer when a Jehovah's Witness rang our doorbell. She smiled sweetly, with her tracts in hand, and said, "I would like to introduce you to the True God." I told her that wasn't necessary since we had already met. Then I shut the door in her face. It wasn't until years later I realized I had been looking in a mirror and didn't know it. This young woman was a model for all the beliefs I had about the nature of religion. My conversion to another religion didn't allow me to escape judging others. Nothing had really changed.

Rabbi Rami Shapiro has said the value of religion is that it preserves examples of the many ways of *da'at d'veikus*, interpreted as the union with God that already exists, but the problem with religion is that it insists only one of these ways is legitimate.[22] Rather than pursue legitimacy with claims of "True God" and "True Religion," it would be more advantageous for me to be humble enough to accept the premise that God is unknowable and beyond comprehension. It is comparable to the five blind men trying to describe an elephant. They all have a part of it but nobody has the whole. If I accept that God is unknowable or beyond the understanding of finite mind, it actually places me in a position of power.

Where does this power originate? One of the purposes of religion, apart from any rituals or cultural traditions, is to increase our consciousness and strengthen our relationship with God and with each other; to move us in the direction of this *da'at d'veikus*. How does this happen? The gradual evolution of the Jewish people advances truth by questioning. Questioning becomes part of the spiritual process, and this is where my power resides. Being able to question is what creates movement on this well-traveled path, one that has lasted thousands of years.

Rabbi Laurence Edwards, Rabbi Emeritus of Congregation Or Chadash, our synagogue that serves the LGBT community of Chicago, phrased this more effectively when he stated, "Judaism is a growing, changing tradition, expansive at its best, embracing, seeking, and unfolding. It shapes us, and it is what we make of it. But it is not simply whatever we say it is. There is a core of teachings, of values, and at that core are questions which must be asked over and over, by each generation."[23]

All too often, religion has become the outer dress or language of the mystical that lies within. The form is often dependent on the particular cultures and civilizations. It is an expression of man's belief about God, yet in most religions, we don't question it. When questioning ceases, the established "core of teachings," which Rabbi Edwards references, withers into strict dogma, a relic that we encase in glass. Religion has to be something I interact with and make real in this physical world. By doing so, I can keep it alive and meaningful. Rabbi Akiva, one of the writers of the Oral Torah or Mishnah,[xxi] stated, "In the eyes of God, personal insight is more precious than Divine Revelation. For if you depend exclusively upon the Scriptures and the teachings of religions and of the masters but have no personal insights of your own, it is all worthless."[24]

We can be such mysterious creatures. We dissolve friendships and disown family members, hate, persecute, and kill one another, and all in the name of this "game" of True Religion. If we can release our religious expectations of each other, we are more connected to each other than we care to admit. Our creaturehood does not

---

xxi   A collection of oral interpretations of the Scriptures from the second century. It forms part of the Talmud, which, in its simplest definition, is a book on rabbinic rulings, or Oral Torah.

conceal any mysteries. We have the same hopes and fears in life, the same desires for our children, and the same search for meaning. We all pray to God, whatever we conceive that to be. What is required is respect, but where has it disappeared to?

The more we approach *da'at d'veikus* we discover that we are as authentic and legitimate as anyone else is, whether that person worships in a synagogue, mosque, or church. Everyone can exist together with no threat to anyone else. We are all here to demonstrate the divine brilliance within us, but we can't accomplish this if we resort to diminishing others by delegitimizing their religious beliefs.

Sadly, the stricter our dogmas become, this wall marked "interpretation of truth" rises higher and stands between us. What we haven't realized yet is that truth is a principle that breaks down when expressed in terms of absolutes. It is dependent on balance for its successful manifestation. When fundamentalist ministers such as Rev. Phelps and his infamous church (a church known for demonstrating at gay pride events and military funerals) bring their religion to town, their demonstration just adds another brick in the wall.

I have read some Hasidic tales that teach certain souls may adopt roles to teach others. By modeling divisiveness and hatred in such extreme measures, is Rev. Phelps acting as a catalyst to prompt us to look within and return to this *da'at d'veikus*? At one protest, which assembled in front of our synagogue, there was one sign from the Presbytery of Chicago that proclaimed, "Presbyterians stand in solidarity with those of all faiths." Maybe things are changing. Maybe we have Rev. Phelps to thank for that.

Right now, what is more valuable than a claim from any religion or denomination being truer or more authentic is our *search* for truth. All of our ancestors experienced God through this search. Exodus, chapter 3, verse 6 states that God said to Moses, "I am… the God of Abraham, the God of Isaac, and the God of Jacob."[25] It would be simpler to write, "I am the God of Abraham, Isaac, and Jacob." So why is the repetition there? Abraham for example, experienced God through the quality of compassion. Isaac viewed God through the quality of judgment (sometimes called discrimination in Kabbalistic literature). Jacob knew God through the synthesis of these qualities. I feel that each of the Patriarchs experienced God in a different way, yet their experiences of God did not challenge or pose a threat to the others.

It should be this way for all of us, here and now. We each experience God differently. The variety of religious theories and practices does not present a threat. In fact, it is refreshing, as we remain open to other viewpoints and continue to explore. Stagnation is the enemy here, not other religions. In spite of the fact that our ancestors may all have experienced God in different ways, and we might experience God differently from them, we are still here. Exodus chapter 3, verse 2 references this continuity through the symbol of the burning bush: "And he [Moses] looked, and here: the bush was burning in the fire, and the bush was not consumed!"[26]

Be Still and Know That I Am God

God is not a result to be obtained but rather an experience.
Arthur

⟅⟆

I can't think of anything more devastating than to experience rejection and isolation from family and friends. That is what happened to Daniel, a young man in a Florida prison, whom I met through the Jews in prison pen pal program, run by the Aleph Institute. The Aleph Institute facilitates contacts between prisoners and those on the outside who wish to establish a pen pal relationship with them. These prisoners have families and friends who have forgotten them, and experience rejection because of the family's shame for the crimes they committed, or for being gay, or both. Some of the prisoners have AIDS, which compounds the problem because of the lack of adequate medical care in the prison system.

After some general letters back and forth, Daniel wrote with a serious question. "Because of what I did, my family has written me off. After thirty-eight years of going against the system the hard way, the answer was right in front of me—God. If only I would have listened sooner. I guess this is the path I had to take to get where I'm going. Did you always believe? Has God always been in your life?"[27]

I wrote back to him with this answer. "God has always been in my life even when I didn't realize He was there. I studied the Scriptures, performed all the required rituals, and thought I knew God. I couldn't find God in the Scriptures (although they do guide me) nor could I find God in the rituals (which, if performed attentively increase my awareness). No, what I needed to do first was reach an understanding of God, an understanding that could only occur when I stopped struggling to find Him.

Imagine a child who excitedly chases a butterfly in the hope of capturing it. Unfortunately, just as the butterfly flies away from the child, God was ever so elusive when I tried to capture Him. The many times I wanted—no, begged—God to help me were the times when my mind was in such turmoil and pain, particularly the years when I couldn't accept myself as gay. How could I possibly have known God's presence when my mental anguish consumed me? No, it is in being still that I make room for Him and provide the terrain that allows me to experience Him. Psalm 46, verse 10 states: "Be still and know that I am God."[28] That was my answer. I could not be still whenever I tried to reason with the conscious mind. It was out of stillness that understanding came.

A child cannot capture the butterfly by wildly chasing it, but if he sits still long enough, the butterfly will rest on a branch or flower and he can know the butterfly's presence. I don't see God as being any different. I cannot explain what is beyond definition. I cannot capture what can only be experienced.

God reveals His presence in my dreams. Shortly after Arthur died, the opportunity to open a metaphysical bookstore in Michigan presented itself to me. I really wanted this. Besides, I had friends in Michigan, and I had grown discontent with city life. I looked at the place, talked to the real estate agent, and considered all my options. I had the money from Arthur's estate, so I figured all the signs were right for me to pursue the project. That night, I dreamt I was driving down a road in a snowstorm. Not being familiar with the road only made the situation worse as I attempted to drive in hazardous conditions. The wind was blowing the snow around faster and faster. It was a very intense dream. I woke up knowing that to buy the shop would be a big mistake. I said no to the agent and my friends, who were quite certain I was going to sign the lease. I have never regretted it.

God dramatically reveals Himself within the events of my life, through themes or patterns, which prompt me to pay attention. It is His way of directing me down a different road. A good example of this is my period of depression and suicidal tendencies. One day I heard a voice within me that said, "Go to church." I heard about the Metropolitan Community Church, a Church with an outreach to gay, lesbian, and transgendered individuals. I went one Sunday and met Arthur there. That chance meeting changed my life. God had His hand in this, and all it took was for me to be still and listen.

It is easy to see God in other people's lives. We often have difficulty seeing Him in ours, particularly when life presents us with what seem to be insurmountable obstacles. If we are still and look closely, we can know Him. We have to start somewhere, no matter how small or insignificant the event."

In 2009, Daniel informed me that someone had asked him to be his sponsor in AA. He was excited about that, and they had long talks together, but he said his protégé didn't get the whole God thing yet, commenting to me, "All I can do is plant the seed."[29] Not long after that, Daniel returned to school within the prison system and reconciled with his mother and son.

Metamorphosis

———

Tmura

The Bridge

If you suffer, it is because of you, if you feel blissful, it is because of you.
Nobody else is responsible.

Osho

Illness was an unwelcome visitor in my childhood. When one ailment finished playing with me, another one appeared to take its place. To be fair, there were times when good health and even vibrant energy manifested. As time passed, those periods were far and few between. My siblings were healthy and didn't present my parents with the challenges that I did. My mother was always worried, as was Dad, but Dad grew more impatient and frustrated with each illness that appeared.

I asked my confessor in the high school seminary one simple question: why is my life filled with such illness? He gave me the same answer previously given to me in grade school. "God's ways are mysterious. God doesn't give you anything you can't handle.

Remember, your suffering is an indication of how much God loves you." I walked away, wishing God would stop loving me so much.

One of the hallmarks of any religion or belief system should be the attainment of a certain peace of mind for the individual. How does my heart feel? Am I at peace? I had to admit I wasn't. At the time, I simply accepted that suffering was punishment, but even so, God was horribly cruel and unjust to inflict it on my life in this manner. I left the seminary with my belief in God shaken, and I became agnostic for a number of years.

I had previously read several books that explored the nature of suffering and tragedy. While they were insightful, some of the authors questioned or gave up their belief in God due to their own personal crises. Shades of bitterness colored the pages so deeply that I wondered whether the authors really wanted to help the reader, or just to share their unresolved anguish. To be fair, the subject of suffering is a complex one. I do have some insights.

My religion focused a lot on the suffering and death of Jesus, and not on the resurrection. It is, in my opinion, a misplaced emphasis. Marianne Williamson, quoting *A Course in Miracles,* states that I should look at the crucifixion, but not dwell on it. I should aspire to the resurrection.[30] Just as Jesus transcended his suffering so that the resurrection could take place, in some small way, I could learn to transcend my life's challenges. Viewed in this manner, suffering is an opportunity rather than a punishment.

When I looked at the suffering of others in this world, I was impressed with how they handled their trials. After seeing the challenges of some people, I certainly preferred to keep my own suffering, even if I was not friends with it yet. Maybe that's where I needed to start—by being friends with it. Friends are often familiar with one another. I was not familiar with my trials. That would require some self-reflection, some meditation, and some prayer. I am not advocating a sterile resignation to suffering. Rather, I think I should experience it and confront it so that ultimately I can become more than who I am. If that approach could take me closer to God, I was willing to try it.

Rabbi Nachman of Breslov has said, "All the world is a very narrow bridge and the most important thing is not to fear at all."[31] I started to view suffering as a bridge that, when I cross it, brings me closer to God. When I can affirm God's presence and respond to Him, that affirmation, that prayer, creates a path, a space so God can walk with me. I will understand that my experience does not exist in a vacuum, separated from Him. Maybe that is the first step on the road to transcendence. I had to learn not to view my experience as separate from a Primal Source because that would generate the fear that paralyzed me, which prevented me from crossing that bridge. No matter what the condition, God cannot operate where there is fear.

So it is not the suffering itself that is critical. It is what I do with it. If I let my suffering define me, where could that possibly take me but toward more suffering? If I believed that life is suffering, it would result in a visual impairment to all the goodness there is in my life. The belief that life itself is suffering is a dangerous one and feeds into a vicious cycle that never ends. Suffering is not an end in itself. That was my problem. I identified with my suffering.

I remember telling Arthur my life was unfair. He shocked me by saying, "All life is fair. You just don't see correctly." So what was "seeing correctly?" He explained that within my illnesses there were a number of possibilities, all having to do with reincarnation. I could be making rectification for errors I had committed in previous lives. Maybe I needed to learn something that only illness could teach. Maybe I just needed to teach someone else to be compassionate through my illness. That last statement was particularly interesting and certainly lends weight to the idea that we are all connected on more levels than we realize.

This concept of reincarnation, or the transmigration of souls, appealed to me tremendously. It shifted the responsibility for my life to me, rather than God. It is a concept not completely relegated to Eastern religion, as there are writings in Judeo-Christian theologies that address this idea.

Carole Devine, a professional astrologer, writer, and lecturer in Norfolk, Virginia, once told me that my health problems stemmed from being overly critical in past lives.[32] If I look back at my life now, I can see where I continued this trend with negative results. In all likelihood, my father modeled this behavior with his constant criticism of me, and I received a chance to experience how I behaved in those past lives. On the other hand, it is probably true that I used criticism as a defense mechanism. I needed somehow to be critical of others before they got a chance to realize how imperfect I was...and judge me. Incorporating Carol's advice to understand that people are imperfect and we all have warts wasn't easy, and yes, I have just started working with this new information, but I am starting to be more relaxed in my approach to life. It is my intention to let life simply be.

I know these ideas push all sorts of emotional buttons for people. As much as reincarnation appealed to me, these ideas pushed the same buttons. I wrestled internally as I continued my discussions with Arthur and the guru at the temple. It certainly forced me to confront my perceptions about the nature of my reality and my beliefs about my personal responsibility in creating it. As time passed, this way of thinking became natural to me.

The rabbi talked about choices, and how I had chosen certain situations before my conception had even occurred. This life is how my soul chose to express itself. Now, I don't necessarily believe that choosing to be gay before conception is a punishment for persecuting gay people in a previous life. Nor does it follow that I incarnated too many times as a female. That sort of reasoning is limiting to me. I am concerned that this sort of rationale goes too deeply into "crime and punishment" again. While it can be true in certain situations, I am leery of absolutes. Suffering is too complex, and to create an absolute on this matter limits the creativity there is in suffering (yes, even in suffering I can be creative). There are as many reasons as there are choices, and the only boundaries to that rule are the ones that I create.

I suppose at some point one can find acceptance, perhaps even a joyous acceptance of their struggles. I am definitely not there yet. I do think that Abraham models what might be called the Zen approach to suffering. In Genesis chapters 23–24, Abraham buries his wife, Sarah, and then proceeds to find a wife for Isaac. The text moves swiftly from one incident to the next. What is not said (and, as is often the case, that is more important than the actual text), is that he surrendered to his suffering and did not let it get in the way of his living. He allowed his suffering to take him to a place where he could see more clearly, by surrendering to it. He accepted his trial without complaint, which in the Talmud is called *vayidom*, based on the Hebrew verb *dome*, to be silent. *Dumah*, from the Aramaic, is silence or stillness. It can also be interpreted to mean, "To hold your peace."

My current circumstances are more than just a reflection of my life in the here and now, and definitely more than a simplified reflection of early childhood abuse. Viewed through a larger lens, my life is a series of pictures of a developing soul, a soul that transcends time. For all is one, all of my lives, and all of them provide input and insight into who and where I am now.

The Resilient Buffalo

Fall down seven times, stand up eight.
Japanese proverb

‏⁓

I wrote the previous chapter, "The Bridge," in 2012. If I thought I had a handle on my emotional response to suffering, I was wrong. In 2013, three herniated cervical disks tested me. The pain was intense, unlike any I had experienced. There was only short-term relief from cortisone shots and physical therapy. The doctors finally recommended cervical spinal fusion surgery, and by the time I received their recommendation, I was almost relieved. Judging from my emotional response to the events, I did not handle it very well. I felt everything I had written in "The Bridge" were words that I had failed to actualize. Was I a hypocrite? No, I just hadn't absorbed the lesson fully. I was just human.

While recuperating from the operation at home, I received a get-well card from Rev. Christine Chakoian, whom I referenced earlier in my introduction. There was a picture of a buffalo on the cover. She wrote on the inside, "The buffalo reminds me of the resiliency embedded in Creation. That which is endangered—whether wild species or human spirit—can be summoned to new resiliency, even in the face of threat."[33]

I started to think about this resiliency in Creation. I think it is resiliency that prompts us, stimulates us, and moves us to respond to the challenges in our lives, and it can take us beyond our own definitions of what is possible. When I reviewed some of my struggles in this light, I felt I was really contacting that resiliency. For example, when I pulled myself out of my suicidal period to go to church, as I talked about in "The First Step," I was responding to the resiliency within me. That action led me to a new place of discovery and healing. When I continued to struggle against the initial adverse effects of HIV and the medications prescribed for it, as I discussed in "The Jacket," I was responding to the resiliency within me that would allow me to shift course and find a different solution.

This resiliency gives birth again to the state of becoming that Daniel Matt explains in *The Essential Kabbalah*.[xxii] He says Creation is "not something completed, but constantly becoming, evolving, ascending. This transports you from a place where there is nothing new to a place where there is nothing old, where everything renews itself, where heaven and earth rejoice as at the moment of Creation."[34]

---

xxii Kabbalah is the mystical interpretation of the Torah. It is a significant part of Hasidism.

We ourselves are Creations, participating with God in this world, but what stops me from participating with Him is when I look at my personal situation and start to define myself by that event or group of events. The illness was only a part of me; it was not me. My pain and suffering was only an aspect of Creation. Yet I hung on to it, rather than move past it and return to the Creative Principle behind its formation.

All too often I don't see the process of Creation as it occurs because I have become so intricately bound to the demands of my everyday life. Daniel Matt, in *God & the Big Bang,* emphasizes the point when he says, "We are enslaved by routines. Rushing from event to event, from one chore to another, we rarely let ourselves pause and notice the splendor right in front of us. Our sense of wonder has shriveled, victimized by our pace of life."[35]

God doesn't exist as an observer, separate from me, but is here within this world as an active participant. When it becomes too difficult to view my life with a sense of wonder anymore, then I need to ask why. There's not going to be a dramatic presentation such as a burning bush, yet in His simplicity, God effectively makes His Presence known. All it takes is a detached perspective, a step back, or a second look around until I become aware of that Presence. I sensed that Presence in my friends who called and offered their support or came to see me after my surgery. I sensed it in Michael, who was with me every step of the way. I was not alone. On the fourth night after surgery, before going to sleep, I was still very weak, but I looked at him and said, "Thank you for being here."

When we move past those events in our lives that test us, challenge us, wear us down, and even threaten us, we can return to the resiliency that resides in all of us. Then a regeneration of spirit and strength forms, which allows us to see the wonder of God's Presence continuously becoming. Perhaps that is what Rev. Chakoian meant when she wrote to me, "May you find within your own soul, the strength of the Creator, whose breath and will, course through you still."[36]

Detachment Takes Place in the Mind

To die, but not to perish, is to be eternally present.
Lao Tzu

When people die of AIDS, why do the newspapers state in their articles, he has "lost his battle with AIDS?" If the mind has an influence over the body, as I believe it does, the emotional impact of words like *battle* could be detrimental to me. As the virus is a part of my physical body now, wouldn't I compromise my immune system by referring to myself in these warlike terms? Don't I inadvertently create a mental construction of resistance and conflict, an atmosphere that can ultimately appear as a weakened immune response or even illness in my physical body?

Since it is so intimately a part of me, I have tried to view my HIV status (I don't care for the word disease) as a lovable part of me that I need to wish well and be at peace with rather than something I need to fight. Louise Hay and others have demonstrated and advanced these ideas in their writings, so this is nothing new.

Another idea that changed my attitude toward illness is the concept of detachment. When I was studying with the rabbi, I told him that new, recently discovered medications had reduced my viral load to zero. He responded, "Certainly the medicine is helping you, but it's your approach to the medication that matters. It's where your mind is. If your focus isn't detached from illness, it doesn't matter what you do on the physical level."

I prefer to adopt the attitude that I need to behave physically as if I have the virus, but to behave mentally as if I don't. If I attached myself mentally to the idea that sickness is inevitable, I would only attract that very situation to myself, regardless of what I was doing in my physical life. It is advantageous, in my opinion, to create a mental space of detachment from sickness and, more importantly, from the fear of sickness.

I know certain souls do take on more challenges, different challenges, than other souls. Their lives are more complicated, as these individuals experience one difficult life event after another. I do think it is the effort extended in facing those challenges that is sometimes more important than the goal itself. A failed effort can do more to promote the growth of my soul when I can surmise what I have learned from that failure. If I am to love God with all my might as Deuteronomy chapter 6, verse 5 states, I must include the idea that my might encompasses all of my efforts, even my failed efforts. I cannot be selective. I cannot discard any part of my life as being irrelevant, failed, or wasted.

It is true that the world only seems to acknowledge efforts that result in visible successes. The outside world will never see my personal efforts in confronting my HIV status. That is as it should be because the focus needs to be on *how* I faced these challenges mentally. A strong mental focus on *how* I travel on the journey makes me a winner every time, and certainly not a second runner up or an "also ran." I honestly think when viewed in this manner, Life or Death becomes irrelevant.

Resolution

Pitaron

Mother's Day

Life is the first gift, love is the second, and understanding the third.
Marge Piercy

When my sister and I went to the funeral home to arrange for Mom's burial, we decided to buy some flowers for Dad's grave. Blue was Dad's favorite color, but for some reason I wanted to buy purple flowers. Purple was Mom's color, and my sister, probably not wanting to provoke an argument, consented. We placed a nice bouquet of purple daisies on Dad's grave. Later I would see how significant this little event was. At that moment, as we made the funeral arrangements, all the events of the past year rose to the surface of my mind.

I remembered how Mom had to learn how to walk again after her operation for ovarian cancer. As I walked with her on the pathway just outside her complex, I couldn't help thinking about the path her own life had taken. The daughter of Italian immigrants, she grew up during the Depression. She once proudly said she had possessed three outfits to her name when she started working, yet she had managed to make do. Yet she was never haughty or snobbish. She raised four children and held down a job at a time when it wasn't fashionable to do so. Her job functioned on several levels. It was important for our family's survival, but it also maintained her sanity. Our father's alcoholism necessitated it.

Mom talked to me as though I were an old friend. The fact is, she was more of a friend than a parent for most of my childhood. Yet she was still my mother, the woman who gave birth to me. She was using a cane, her other hand held tightly to mine as we slowly walked down the concrete path together. This picture of dependency was foreign to my experience of her, as she hesitated to ask people for help. She was struggling to begin again. Gradually she did feel stronger and was walking without the cane, visiting with her friends, and shopping. I took her wherever she wanted to go, which was usually shopping. When she wanted to shop, I knew her energy had returned. Then I had the dream.

Dream journal entry June 21, 2000

Mom was lying on this big round bed, talking gently to me. She said, "I'm not going to make it. I won't last another year. Come here." She scooped me up and held me in her arms. "I used to hold you like this in my bed when you were a child." She continued to hold me, saying, "There now, isn't this wonderful?" There was a definite peacefulness to it, bliss. Here I was, an adult male in bed with my mother, yet there was nothing incestuous about it. I knew the circular bed represented infinity and at the time, I felt as if our two souls were communicating one last time to each other. The feeling was euphoric. She was right; it was "wonderful."

Ultimately, nothing about the dream really shocked me. As I mentioned in "Walking with a Limp," studying reincarnation and my past lives helped me connect with our history together. I recognized several lives that explained our strong connections. We were mother and son, husband and wife, in several lives. We were good friends in others. The friendship part bled through strongly in this life, for not only was she my mother, she was my best friend.

Now that I think of it, the violation of boundaries that she perpetuated with me as a child, while it was *still a violation in this life*, was also behavior stemming from past-life remembrances of more intimate relationships. The remembrance of our past-life roles seeped through and influenced our current ones. Those roles were entirely inappropriate for the situation. It does explain why it was so easy for me to confront her the way I did. I remember a birthday card she sent me that was more poignant than anything she could have said to me. The card read, "I've always loved you, even before you were born." I still have that card.

Mom eventually returned to the hospital because of a blood clot that doctors were concerned might travel to her heart or her brain. She was under orders to remain in bed to allow the swelling in her leg to recede. People came to visit her most of the day, friends, family, and, of course, the nurses and doctors. Finally, when we were alone, I pulled the curtain to give us some privacy and told her I wanted to talk to her. I said I loved her very much and I asked her to forgive me for any pain that I might have caused her. She just looked straight ahead. At first, I thought she didn't hear me. Finally she answered, "There's nothing to forgive."

As time passed, I watched her condition eventually worsen during that year. I remembered the dream but never said anything to my siblings for fear I could be wrong (or maybe it was out of fear I could be right). She slipped back into ill health, until the final diagnosis came from her doctor that he could do nothing more. Faced with the inevitable, she consented to enter hospice. She even refused to let my older brother sign the papers on her behalf, and dragged herself out of bed to do so. My siblings and I established hospice in her bedroom.

She couldn't feed herself anymore and asked me to do so. I was intent on making her comfortable; keeping her level of pain down; seeing that she had whatever she might want. We were the only two people in the room at that time, but we might as well have been the only two people in the universe. She wasn't speaking much, but our eyes met soul to soul, rather than mother to son. In that timeless moment, I felt connected to God. I later realized it was one of the few times I wasn't biting my lip to keep from crying. Thoughts of my own personal pain had vanished.

On the fourth day of hospice, I awoke and went in immediately to say hello and see how her night had been. She recognized me and said "hi." That was it. "Hi" was the last word she ever said to me. My longing to hear her speak again was only partially satisfied when I saw she could still recognize us. We stayed with her, ready to help if needed. The reality of it was we felt helpless; she was starting the final leg of a journey that she needed to travel alone.

A stream of relatives visited over the weekend, saying their goodbyes. It was the sixth night of hospice. I slept on the couch in the living room, although I wouldn't exactly call it sleep. I would doze, briefly wake up, and doze off again. I thought at times I heard her, but she had stopped talking two days ago, so I dismissed that idea. She died on April 1, the seventh night of hospice, ten months later, fulfilling my dream.

At the funeral, a friend remarked that when a soul realizes it is time to leave, it will start withdrawing from the activities of this earthly life, losing interest in the outside world and eventually refusing to eat or drink or speak. That was certainly true in Mom's case. I didn't recognize the event for what it was, as I was too absorbed in my own pain. I don't think I would have felt so bad if I was aware of that when she was in hospice.

Three days after Mom's burial, a local florist delivered flowers from some friends in Florida to our home. The card attached said "Congratulations!" The florist must have realized what he had done because five minutes later the deliveryman was back. When I opened the door he immediately declared, "I was told you were to have these." I thanked him, shut the door, and searched for a vase. I froze when I opened the tissue and looked at the flowers; there were three pink roses nestled in a bouquet of purple daisies. I knew without a doubt Mom sent those flowers to me, for you see, my mother's name was Rose. It was her way of saying "I'm okay." Implicit in her message was "…and you will be too."

Some people have said it is coincidence; a few have told me I am naïve. Others have just accepted it as my belief. It is not belief but a simple knowledge that has no basis other than itself. I simply know. Consciousness always seeks to express itself even when it crosses over to the other side. It is a great comfort to know the soul wants to communicate its survival.

It has been twelve years since she died. That's either a long time or just yesterday, depending on where I am psychologically. But every year on Mother's Day I visit her grave to say hi and to bring her pink roses and purple daisies.

Melissa Ann

Nothing is ever really lost to us as long as we remember it.
L.M. Montgomery

This is the story of Melissa Ann. That's what her tag said, but we just called her Melissa. She was in our mother's night-stand when we were cleaning up after she died. My sister took one look at her and said, almost to herself, "Now what the heck was she saving this for?" My younger brother, who is usually more direct, made a face, laughed, and said, "God, is she ugly!" I had to agree with him.

Melissa is a doll, not more than seven inches high. She wears a short knitted dress decorated with a butterfly and a ladybug. Cotton fills her body, her arms short and stubby in comparison with her legs, which are very long. Oh, and did I mention she has two antennae sticking out from her head?

We used to help Mom go through her belongings every so often, so we knew what she had, and we had never seen Melissa before. We also knew her taste, and Melissa was not something she would collect. It must have been a recent purchase. We really had no other explanation. Maybe she bought it on the street from some vendor. Mom couldn't say no to someone in need. In any event, we didn't have the heart to throw Melissa out, and while my older brother took her back home to Maryland, she really stayed with all of us.

She started making appearances in the family, showing up as the additional Christmas or birthday gift to each other. When that became tiresome, we took to slipping her into one another's homes without the other's knowledge. As time passed, we would forget about her. Then someone would ask, "Who has Melissa?" Two years ago, when my brother was in town for a family funeral, he, with the help of my sister and sister-in-law, slipped her into one of the drawers in our coffee table without my knowledge, and notified me after he left that a "visitor" was still in our home. Even after he revealed what he did and sent hints by e-mail regarding her location, I still couldn't find her.

I suppose we had cried so much before Mom had even died that we needed to find a release mechanism, and Melissa filled the bill. Maybe God sent her to us to comfort us. Melissa was a way for us to laugh and remember Mom. She loved a good joke. She was probably watching us all this time and laughing along with us.

On March 17, Michael threw a party for me in honor of my sixtieth birthday with family and friends. My older brother returned Melissa to me in a silver mesh box. She sits on my desk now as inspiration, and I've decided that is where she will stay. While her story probably doesn't contain the wisdom of some of the Bible stories and rabbinic legends that have passed from generation to generation, it's no less important. In our memories are our blessings. Whatever possessed our mother to buy this ugly little doll, Melissa is certainly a physical symbol of our connection to her and the love we had for her. And *that* makes Melissa beautiful.

What Can I Say About My Father?

No matter how much you would like to feel
sorry for yourself, your life is still your responsibility.
Old Indian (*Poltergeist II*)

Studying the Ten Commandments in grade school, I remembered learning that the fifth commandment was "You shall love your father and mother." I always had a problem with that one because my father was the last person whom I felt should be deserving of my love. That is putting it bluntly, but it's true. Years later, I discovered that the actual translation of the commandment was "You shall *honor* your father and mother." Whether the correct word was love or honor, the only thing I could give my father was undying hatred because of his verbal, emotional, and physical abuse of me.

When I started to study Kabbalah, the rabbi told me in a private lesson, "You chose your father, you know. You chose a father who beat you up so he could toughen you up. You needed someone to toughen you up because your soul was weak. He wanted you to react, to fight back, and he was willing to risk your alienation for that. He did it to help you survive."

As I learned from several therapists, surviving my childhood meant repressing large pieces of it. It is comparable to post-traumatic stress disorder. In order to transcend the abuse, I went somewhere else mentally when Dad hit me. I survived by not remembering very much. All I had left were flashes of memories too fleeting for me to assemble into any meaningful picture. Some memories flowed to the surface of my awareness again, appearing at what I thought were odd or inconvenient times, and I learned how to experience the feelings without having them destroy me.

When I wrote my mother's eulogy, I discovered it gave me a wonderful perspective on her life. Dad had died nineteen years earlier, and I thought the passage of time would only help me achieve a similar perspective. I was wrong. I didn't count on the difficulties of putting those memories to paper. What abusive events I did remember from my childhood were absent. I hadn't recounted a single episode of abuse. Only the good memories appeared in the following eulogy I wrote for him. How was that possible?

What can I say about my father? These are the things I remember...

I remember all the meals he prepared for us. He had been a cook during his army service, and he put his training to good use in preparing our meals. Sunday was donuts...from scratch. Monday was pizza...from scratch, not to mention chicken and roast beef on other days of the week. He loved to cook, and he was good at it.

He built our house from the ground up: the walls, flooring, insulation, plumbing, and electricity. I was five at the time, and he perched me on a secure floorboard in the half-finished attic so I could watch him and his brothers and in-laws install the rest of the floor. The one bedroom he constructed on the second floor was mine after my older brother left for college.

He was also very creative. On a fall day in October, I heard noise in the garage and wandered into it. Dad was there, sawing some wood pieces. I was eight at the time; I asked very simply, "Dad, what are you doing?" He wiped the dust off his face as it was still floating around him. "Aww, I was making your Christmas gift, but I tell you what. I will make this for you now, and I'll give you another gift at Christmas."

He proceeded to show me all the wooden pieces he had sawed and how he was going to assemble them into a pinball game. The game itself used one-inch marbles. The pull was an old brass spindle from a lamp. The frame was solid wood with a tray at the bottom to collect the marbles after they had spun their way around the pins he had carefully inserted.

There were the original house decorations he constructed for us at Christmas. One year he created a plywood Santa and three reindeer, painted them, and even attached a red electrical light to Rudolph's nose. Electrical conduit, bent with his wrenches, formed the sled runners. That rooftop display won second-best decorated house in the village one year (although to my child mind, I couldn't imagine anything better than Santa and his reindeer on our roof possibly winning first prize).

The train sets Dad created were mesmerizing. I've never seen anything like them. One year he had three trains running on three different levels, and these were the Lionel 0–27 gauge trains, so the display that year occupied one third of our living room. The whole setup had a console off to the side with three transformers, and even switches so you could divert the trains along different sections of the tracks.

With paint and plywood and dollhouse accessories and train novelties, he would construct whole villages populated with miniature cutouts of people. Cars "traveled" the painted roads, dotted by telephone poles strung with wire. At certain points on the route, the train could stop and little specialized cars could drop off milk cartons on a loading dock or herd miniature cattle to a corral.

Dad was talented, and he worked hard at whatever he did. I had no concept back then just how hard he worked. My work ethic came from him, though, and he was a wonderful example.

Most of all I remember how he, not my Mom, was the first one at my side when I had my seizures. He caught me before I fell down the stairs or otherwise hurt myself, took me back to bed, and tucked me in again. My seizures were one of the few times when his gentleness surfaced. I cling to those memories because his displays of affection were so intermittent.

While Dad's displays of affection were few, I realized that he had difficulty expressing himself. Dad, rough on the exterior, was a sensitive soul. Sometimes sensitive people protect themselves from being hurt, and alcohol was his protection, the drug that numbed his pain. I was never completely aware of the source of his pain, but it must have been difficult growing up as one of the youngest of ten siblings.

Marianne Williamson has said that the ego is so invested in being right, it can only see what the parent did wrong.[37] That is true, because for everything he did wrong, there was a lot he did that was right. One of the things he did right as a father was to accept me as his son, even after I revealed I was gay. While I heard of other fathers rejecting their children because of their sexuality, that was never an issue with him.

I didn't see any of these qualities at the time because, as Alan Morinis states in his book, *Everyday Holiness,* I saw "only his flaws and failings." I focused on the exterior soiled garments rather than the divinely inspired being that my father was.[38] There was something within him, strength, a resolve, a refusal to give up completely; for as often as he picked up the bottle, he put it down, even holding down two jobs for a number of years to support us. Only time brought back that memory and gave me a more balanced perspective.

So, what can I say about my father except that I remember him with love and compassion now, but also with regret. I regret he wasn't able to show his love more readily and make himself vulnerable to his children. I regret, as an adult, laying expectations on him that he couldn't possibly fulfill. Then I regret all the lost time and lost chances I washed away with my anger. I regret not being able to rise above my hurt and see him for who he was. Now that I have this perspective, he's not here to talk to, at least not in a way that I would like. Most of all, I regret that I wasn't able to see the goodness within him until it was almost too late. But I did see it, and as well as I could at the time, we did patch things up. Dad showed me how to be strong and persevere. It is the demonstration of that strength that made him a hero. Yes, I have given up many times, and have despaired on several occasions. As I slipped and stumbled with the events of life, I always climbed back and returned. I guess my strength was my father's gift to me. The rabbi was right, after all…

With death comes the end of physical pain. I believe that death does not extinguish the personality, but only helps it to grow. I can only pray that Dad has now reconciled within himself his pain and has moved beyond it. More importantly, perhaps Dad sees how important his efforts were to me, who he had a hand in creating, and how much he was loved for having done so.

A significant dream revealed itself shortly after he died. Dad was in the hallway of my childhood home, and I told him, "What's going on between us has to stop." I remember the intensity of his blue eyes as he replied, "I will if you will." It was becoming clearer. I had a hand in this relationship, too. Every time I escaped responsibility for my actions by loudly proclaiming, "Well, I am a victim of my father's abuse," in some small measure I kept the old hatreds alive. My attachment to him perpetuated itself, and the peace that could have been mine would always be elusive because I wouldn't forgive him. Besides, wearing the cloak of victimhood looked ludicrous on a sixty-one-year-old male. When would I have enough? I needed to release him so that both of us would be free again.

That release came from a memory of one of my college classmates, Chris. He had been away from school for a week to attend his father's funeral. I expressed my sympathies, but he quickly cut me off, saying, "Don't bother. He was a bastard." On some level, I was still the same way with Dad. I really didn't want to be that person anymore.

In his book *God is a Verb*, Rabbi David A. Cooper tells a short story in which God assigns an angel the task of finding the best quality of human experience. After several tries, the angel discovers that quality is forgiveness. And God says, "…this is one of the few traits that distinguish human potential. Without forgiveness, all Creation would disappear in an instantaneous flash."[39]

I don't remember exactly when the change occurred, but I found myself defending Dad to others who criticized him. Or I found myself wishing the indecisive people in my life could be more decisive, just like my father! That wasn't typical of me in the past and certainly indicated a shift in thinking. Then there were times when sadness engulfed me because I missed him and wanted to see him again. If I believe the words which I have written in "The Value of Goodness," then he, too, was a good man. Really.

The Commandments are not a bunch of words engraved in stone. These words are living forces that carry the creative impetus we read about in Genesis, chapter 1, verse 3, when God said "*Yehi Or, let there be light…*"[40] These principles thrust themselves forward whether I choose to embrace them into my life or sit passively and just study them. Just because my parents are no longer here, I cannot shelve the fifth commandment and say, "Well, this one doesn't apply anymore." I still have the opportunity (and the obligation) to observe it. It is who I become, here and now, that brings honor to my parents. Releasing Dad from being responsible for my actions as an adult is probably the best way I can think of to honor my father, and to fulfill the commandment "You shall honor your father and mother."

I love you, Dad. Rest in peace now.

I Remember

When you remember me, it means that you have carried something of who I am with you...
Frederick Buechner

⁓

After Mom's funeral was over and everyone returned to his or her own life, I was alone to face the fact that my last parent had died. I remember reading a book called *The Orphaned Adult*, by Alexander Levy. The title was exactly how I felt: an orphan.

As if to emphasize the point, one Friday evening, a visiting rabbi presented a talk on the Jews in China to our synagogue. He had asked one of the Chinese citizens there who was more important, the parent or the child. His response was "The parent of course. The possibility exists to have another child. You can never have another parent."

Even though Dad abused me and Mom enabled him, it was still an adjustment to realize they were both gone. No matter where we had left things, our relationship on the physical level was over. Our machzor for the High Holidays contains a poem by Linda Pastan, entitled "For a Parent," part of which reads:

> Move to the front
> of the line
> a voice says, and suddenly
> there is nobody
> left standing between you
> and the world, to take
> the first blows on their shoulders.
> This is the place in books
> where part one ends, and
> part two begins,
> and there is no part three…[41]

So what happens now? All I have are my memories. They were a two-edged sword, painful and pleasant. Time softened those memories and dulled the rough edges of the more painful ones. My memories helped me piece together a more complete picture of who my parents were. The painful times gradually subsided. The pleasant times resurfaced, reminding me there were good memories, even if they had been submerged or shoved aside temporarily. I realized that what I chose to remember held the greatest value.

As time has passed, my relationship with my parents feels nebulous now, as if they never existed. Yet I can turn the corner of a street, see roses in a neighbor's yard, and Mom returns in sharp focus. I can see a cardinal, and Dad immediately comes into my mind (he loved cardinals). My relationship with my parents is stronger than ever when those memories surface because those memories make them real again, even if they are not physically present.

This poem by an unknown author accurately describes my feelings:

> In many houses, all at once
> I see my mother and father
> and they are young as they walk in.
> Why should my tears come, to see them laughing?
> That they cannot see me is of no matter.
> I was once their dream; now they are mine.[42]

New Beginnings /
Starting Over

⸺

Hatchala Chadasha

Abracadabra

Remember that you must build your life as if it were a work of art.
Rabbi Abraham Joshua Heschel

⸺

When I was young, I watched a magician on television. He showed the audience an empty black hat, waved his hand over it, and pronounced the magic word, *"Abracadabra!"* Then he would pull a rabbit out of his hat. The word *abracadabra* originates from the Hebrew *evrah kedabri*, literally, "having spoken, it occurred," or "I will create as I speak," or the Aramaic phrase *avra kehdabra*, meaning, "I create by speaking."

The first example of Creation by speaking is obviously in Genesis, where in chapter 1, verse 3, God says, "Yehi Or, let there be light, and there was light."[43] In the subsequent passages of Genesis, we see the repetition of the phrase, "And God said, 'Let there be…'" for the remaining six days of Creation. So, while the word *abracadabra* might evoke the image of a magician pulling a rabbit out of his hat, it carries a warning of the power, and obligation, to speak responsibly, for the word is the manner by which Creation takes place in the world.

Christianity offers many examples of Jesus creating by speaking, whether by healing the sick, or raising the dead, all with a simple spoken command. One obvious example is in the Gospel of Matthew, chapter 8, Verse 5–8. A Roman centurion asks for help for his servant who is "lying at home paralyzed, in terrible distress." Jesus said to him, "I will come and cure him."[44] The centurion's response, in effect, is "You don't need to do that. All you have to do is speak and I know it will happen."

One of Creation's major qualities is the impetus to continually become more than what it is. Rabbi Rami Shapiro, in his annotations of *Hasidic Tales*, remarks that God Himself is "infinite becoming, arising from infinite being."[45] Judaism follows that same path of continually becoming, evidenced by a vast library of sources from revered writers such as Moses, Rabbi Akiva, the RamBam,[xxiii] the Baal Shem Tov, and others, words that exist to this day. Yet Creation by speaking follows paths that are at times marked by detours into religious fanaticism and hateful speech. Like our respected sages and scholars, long after the people or cultures involved have disappeared, the erroneous hate-filled documents continue to exist, and they, too, have a life of their own.

Rabbi Gershon Winkler states, "You are Creation in process, a flower unfolding, a seed sprouting." This consciousness is known as the Sacred Walk. Referencing Genesis 17:1, he states, "God says,

---

xxiii Acronym for Rabbi Moshe ben Maimon. Also known as Maimonides (son of "Maimon"), Maimonides was a twelfth-century philosopher and physician.

'Walk before me and be both simple and whole.'"[46] Being both simple and whole, however, is not such an easy proposition where speech is concerned. We learn from a few instances in the Torah that Jacob had to confront his words of deception to his father, Isaac, by having to experience deception at the hands of Laban when he discovered he was married to Leah, instead of Rachel. Miriam must confront the effects of her *lashon hora*,[xxiv] or derogatory speech, through leprosy after she speaks ill of her younger brother Moses.

I may be a sprouting seed according to Rabbi Winkler, but through my words, I can assert that some of those sprouts have grown into something I didn't intend. As a creature of habit, it becomes so easy for me to create by speaking without thinking. I wonder, if I were more fully conscious when I spoke, might I remember to ask myself, will my words destroy or create?

The Hasidic story about a gossip who slandered his rabbi comes to mind. The rabbi met with the gossip who asked for forgiveness. As part of his penance, he returned home, took a feather pillow and ripped it up, scattering the feathers to the four winds. When he returned, the rabbi told him to go back and retrieve the feathers.

"But that's impossible," the man said. "Precisely," the rabbi answered. "And although you sincerely regret the damage you have done me, it is as impossible to undo it as it is to recover all the feathers."[47]

---

xxiv Literally "evil talk" or "evil tongue," the concept of slanderous, derogatory speech about another person.

I recognize I have lost friendships due to ill-chosen words. I recognize I have lost my temper because of my impaired internal boundaries. Words sailed off my tongue on the winds of emotion that I could not retrieve. It is daunting to realize how accurate the words of Rabbi Abraham Joshua Heschel are when he said, "Know that… every word is power…"[48] I don't realize that when I say something it becomes a living thing that stands on its own, generating effects of which I am oblivious.

I remember a man who was oblivious to what he created. When I was able to drive, I took Mom card shopping at Wieboldt's, a popular department store. We overheard an elderly couple in the same aisle. The wife said, "Now, I want to buy a wedding card for your nephew. Isn't it wonderful he's getting married after all these years?" I remember the husband, not pleased to be tagging along with his wife, staring straight ahead and rocking on his heels. He replied in a droll voice, "The sympathy cards are in the next aisle."

We burst out laughing, but abruptly stopped when the man turned to us and said, "I saw you laughing. You thought that was funny, didn't you?" Then he winked, and smiled as if to say, "Yeah, I thought it was funny, too." After that, at family get-togethers when relatives would swap stories, Mom would bring up the "Wieboldt's Man," as she called him, and start laughing all over again.

About a week before she died, I was sitting on the edge of Mom's bed, in conversation with her, when she quietly asked, "Do you remember…that man in Wieboldt's? That was funny." She couldn't laugh this time, but she remembered…and she smiled. The Wieboldt's man probably went home and continued his life, with hardly a thought of us. But he created, by speaking, a moment in time that she never forgot, even though it may have been small and insignificant to him. Again, "Know that…every word is power…"[49]

So, all the angry words I threw at Dad, Mom, and my siblings stepped forward to confront me again. If words are power, what had I done with that power? What had I created? When I look back, I cringe at some of the things I said to them as well as to others. No matter how small or insignificant it may seem, everything I say is important. How much better it is to build something constructive with my words. If I was really going to change, that change needed to start with being more conscious of my words.

The Creation that started in Genesis continues to move forward in time through me, whether I consciously cooperate with it or not. Creation is all around. If I stop long enough to observe the world around me, I can see the effects of my words, my "Creation by speaking," in the damage my hurtful comments have made, or the pain that my angry tone can generate. I can also hear those effects of Creation through words in our grandchildren's spontaneous expressions of joy when they see us. Creation resides in kind words given in a spirit of compassion. I can feel it in Michael's words of comfort, in an attempt to alleviate my pain. I can even laugh with Creation in a humorous story, which, years later, surfaces in a memory to momentarily ease a dying woman's pain.

Abracadabra.

The Value of Goodness

True goodness springs from a man's own heart. All men are born good.
Confucius

When I returned for my second year of seminary, I met a new classmate. John was an energetic, boisterous young man who had a comment for everything, whether about our classmates or the priests. It was particularly annoying because his running commentary distracted me.

One morning, Father told us, "OK, class, your writing assignment today is to describe yourself in twenty-five words or less." John leaned back in his chair, folded his arms, and bragged, "Hey, Father, that's easy. I could describe myself in twenty-five words." I muttered under my breath, "Hell, I could describe you in one word." Only I didn't use the word *hell*. I was so sure no one heard me. A solitary comment, and I'm the one sent to the Dean's office…

That is a challenging assignment, isn't it? If you could only use one word to describe yourself, what word would it be? Think about it. Is there a word that describes you? Or would you find that one word defines an aspect of you, but does not fully encompass all that you are?

I decided to try it. Like a painter with a blank canvas, I threw words on a mental slate only to end up erasing them; feeling frustrated because none of them really described the person who I was. I started using the declarative I AM to help the discovery process. I came up with I AM introverted, serious, intense, and perfectionistic. Then the negatives showed up: I AM obsessive, temperamental, impatient, and critical. It made sense that my mind would move to the opposite side of the spectrum, and while all of these words were true to one extent or another, they didn't capture my essence.

I withdrew mentally and tried to find a word that dug into the roots of who I was as a soul. I said I AM loveable. That felt better, but I wasn't satisfied. No, I needed to find a word that really couldn't be challenged. I came up with I AM…good! Genesis chapter 1, verse 27 states, "…God created man in His own image…" and in Genesis 1, verse 31, "And God saw everything that He had made, and behold it was very good."[50] No matter what words I use to define myself, I must start with the first word, and that is good.

That was difficult, for Dad's favorite words to me were, "You're no good." Naturally, I carried that belief into adulthood. I needed to reverse that belief by embracing the idea I can have flaws, I can stumble, I can fall and make mistakes, but that does not alter my goodness. Goodness is who I am.

I Am a Jew

Shema Yisrael, Adonai Eloheinu Adonai Echad!
(Hear O Israel, the Lord is our God, the Lord is One!)[xxv]

$$\sim$$

I changed residences fourteen times over the course of sixteen years before I met Michael. It wasn't that I couldn't find a physical home. It was that I couldn't find a spiritual one. My continual moving was a reflection of the internal searching inside of me. There was restlessness inside of me I couldn't define back then.

For all the ideas and concepts we discussed over the course of our time together, Arthur never said anything about Judaism, only remarking that he knew very little about it. One day he told me, "I have started to read this book about Kabbalah. I think you should study it." Then, rather cryptically, he added, "I'm not going to

---

xxv The central prayer of faith for all Jews. It declares belief in one God.

have the time." I didn't attach any importance to his remark, but I remembered it when he died less than a year later.

I did start to study Kabbalah after he died, only to quickly drop it for a number of reasons, the main one being that I did not have any knowledge or understanding of the rites and rituals of Judaism. The significance of Kaballah was lost on me without this necessary component. By studying Kaballah first, I had entered through the back door, if you will, and it didn't work.

A year after that, I met Michael. He invited me to dinner Friday night, and I asked him, "What are these blessings you say? What are your rituals? What is your culture? Tell me about your religion." He explained all that and more to me. He took me to Or Chadash, our synagogue, in 1992, and we have been there ever since.

There, I learned about Judaism through our friends and our first rabbi, Suzanne Griffel. She also taught me how to write a d'var. I met Carol Goldbaum, a longtime member who has held several positions on the board. She taught me to blow the shofar.[xxvi] There I was, in a welcoming environment, similar to the Metropolitan Community Church I had attended in my twenties.

Hebrew was foreign to me, obviously, yet it felt familiar, if that makes any sense. The language, the ritual, all had beauty within them. However, it was the precepts of Judaism, and the ethics, that challenged me. I remembered that feeling. It was the same feeling I'd had when talking with Arthur. I may not have had a personal

---

xxvi A ritual instrument made from a ram's horn. It is blown primarily on the Jewish New Year, although it can be used to announce the new moon and to call people together.

Teacher who challenged me in the same way my Taoist friend did, but Judaism actually became my Teacher.

As time passed, and Michael opened his heart to me, I knew just how good a man he was. I would never have experienced that goodness if I had not previously declared my own (as I wrote about in "The Value of Goodness"). I realized that figuratively speaking, Michael had stepped into my life so he could take me home. And I was home. God always tells me where I need to be if I can listen, and I listened that night. I had passed out of the shadow of the darkness of my longing. I was ready to settle down. I was ready to begin.

What's in a Name?

Accept no one's definition of your life, but define yourself.
Harvey Fierstein

⟋‿⟍

I really hated the name I received at birth. In my teens, I entertained using other names by researching them, trying them on as if I were purchasing a fancy suit. However, I soon dismissed the idea of a name change and regarded it as a silly desire. Mom gave me my birth name anyway, so I did not want to hurt her feelings. When I converted to Judaism, the idea of a change in name resurfaced. It would certainly be appropriate because it would be a way of affirming my new identity, wouldn't it? Joel or Joshua were two of the names I thought of using, but ultimately they just didn't feel right. So I released the idea again.

Eight more years passed, and I was attending a seminar on Kabbalah in the spring. The rabbi was talking about the significance of Passover. Attendance was low, so he had time for a few personal questions with each attendee. I asked him, if I wanted to change my name, how would I find the right name for me, or, to be more specific, for my soul? This was his answer: "Go home and just before going to bed, read *Chayei Sarah*.[xxvii] You will have a dream tonight which will give you your name."

And I did. In my dream, I was in my bed sleeping with a young dog. The dog turned into a lion. I woke up. That was it. It was a simple dream, but it made no sense to me at the time. Now, I had just purchased the midrash on Genesis during that week, and started to read it that day. Jacob is on his deathbed, blessing his sons, and when he comes to Yehuda, he says, "A whelp (young cub or dog) and a lion is Yehuda."[51] The Torah portion commentary for *Va-Yihi*, which recounts the same story, states that the phrase is a metaphor for strength, daring, and invincibility. I eventually understood that strength is a matter of gradual transformation. I had to learn slowly how to move into greater strength, the strength of a lion. It was not so much a physical transformation as it was a spiritual one.

Yehuda is associated with the Tribe of Kings, from which King David descended, and Malkuth, the tenth and lowest of the Sefirot,[xxviii] which, interestingly enough, is associated with the mouth. The mouth ultimately becomes a creator or a destroyer, depending on how I use it. If I am honest with myself, I "created by speaking" more dissension in my life by using my mouth inappropriately. I did a lot of criticizing; I made many judgments.

---

xxvii Chayei Sarah is the Torah portion that starts with the death of Sarah and follows Abraham as he adjusts to her passing and finds a wife for Isaac.

xxviii According to Jewish mysticism, Sefirot are the ten emanations by which God manifests in the world.

The last name did not come as easily. I struggled with various names and became frustrated because nothing seemed to fit. I wanted to take Michael's last name, but he quickly nixed that idea, saying I should have a name that is mine. I eventually agreed with him. The answer came about in an indirect way. A good friend of mine dreamt that we were at a party and wanted to introduce me, but didn't know my last name. Someone came to him and said, "Tell him his name is Jacobi, and it is to be spelled J-a-c-o-b-i." Having heard my friend's dream, I knew my prayer was answered.

Jacobi is "from or of the House of Jacob." Jacob is the most obvious example of a name change in the Torah outside of Abraham and Sarah. Jacob was renamed Israel after wrestling with the angel. I think his name change reflects changes in identity and shifts in consciousness. Jacob was a changed man after his encounter with the angel, both physically and spiritually.

I chose Raphael as my Hebrew name when I converted because it was the Hebrew name of my father, who had died the previous year. Raphael is one of the archangels and means "God who has healed" or "Healer." This had significant meaning, considering our contentious and fractured relationship.

Over time, the meanings of the three names linked themselves together into one central thought: "The creation of healing in a balanced manner through the judicious use of the mouth." I see this statement as a goal to achieve and certainly not a statement of accomplishment. It is raw potential to aspire to and to activate. I view it as a chance to reinvent myself.

My old name served its purpose, but it is not me anymore. It does not serve my life as I live it now. I love my new name, and I never look back in regret over my decision. It feels comfortable, it feels right, and it has a rhythm to which I respond. I have found my name.

Afterword

Truly, the greatest gift you have to give is that of your own self-transformation.
Lao Tzu

Each of the categories in this book (Boundaries, Confrontation, Judgment, etc.), may appear to the reader as separate pieces, but they are parts of a cohesive whole. It is important to add that these categories functioned together, at the same time, with varying degrees of clarity for me, even if I isolated them on the pages within this book.

One common thread in many of the pieces is the theme of fear. I don't think I could confront my fears without the vulnerability I expressed in this book. That vulnerability was my asset. The fears themselves, though, were an illusion. After years of effort, the major breakthrough for me was the understanding that *it was never really about me.* Dad's cruelty was a projection of himself.

He was reacting from his own fear of "not being good enough," a fear of inadequacy that he took with him into adulthood. I understand now that he was in so much pain and didn't know how to handle it. I learned from family members that his parents did not treat him very well. He was the ninth of eleven children, and I suppose at that point, his parents just didn't have the time or the patience for their younger children. He had a brother, Tom, who was epileptic, like me. His parents favored him so strongly that when Dad came back from his service in the army they had given all his civilian clothes to Tom.

How could my father not react the way he had when shadows of his childhood, like me, confronted him on a daily basis? I was the materialization of his fears in a very metaphysical sense. Even though it took me this long to realize it, he chose me just as much as I chose him. By presenting myself as a symbol of his past, I offered him the opportunity to forgive his brother, something he needed to confront. I do think he knows that now. I was there to teach him just as much as he taught me. It may not be as simple as that, as my reasons for being on this earth encompass several levels, but I do think there is an element of truth to the statement.

I no longer choose to call myself a victim. It is true that I still deal with the psychological effects of my childhood, but I no longer blame my parents for it. They raised me according to the way their parents raised them. I know I am rough around the edges (not unlike Dad). I am difficult to know, and I'm certainly not perfect, but that's OK. I am a good man. I have value and I have a right to be here.

My early years focused on surviving, and with the help of therapy, healing. Initially, I bounced from one crisis to another, whether it was health or family, friends or employers. My focus now is on thriving. I learned how to create family, friends, and employers who support me. I learned how to remove myself from the energy of situations that don't affirm my goodness. I have traveled more, allowing myself to experience more of the world. I have continued my studies in religion, particularly Kabbalah.

Goodness and joy appear now with more regularity. One Sunday, we were reading the papers with our coffee on the patio. I happened to look up, and all around me. I saw the brightness of the sun and the flowers I had planted in the spring blooming in the garden. I saw Michael, absorbed in his section of the paper. I remembered to be grateful for it all, and I returned to the paper thinking, "This is nice. This is very nice. I deserve this."

I had finished this afterword when, only a week later, I had the following dream.

Dream journal entry May 21, 2013

I dreamt I was dying. There was a little boy with curly, reddish hair standing in front of me. I looked into his eyes as I took him by the hands. He looked at me very simply and sensed my impending death. I remembered telling him, "You are so precious. I want to tell you how special you are to me. I hope that someday you will find someone who is as special to you as you are to me."

The boy, to me, represented the innocence of youth. He was just beginning his life. After some reflection, I realized I was talking to a potential self of mine. Part of me was dying and my death in the dream indicated a transition from who I was to who I could be. As I stated before in the text, and as the dream indicates, life is a continual journey.

Additional Inspirational Reading

Mitch Albom, *The Five People You Meet in Heaven.* (New York: Hyperion, 2003).

Noah benShea, *Jacob the Baker: Gentle Wisdom for a Complicated World.* (New York: Ballantine Books, 1989).

Noah benShea, *Jacob's Journey: Wisdom to Find the Way, Strength to Carry On.* (New York: Ballantine Books, 1991).

Rabbi Philip S. Berg, *Kabbalistic Astrology Made Easy.* (New York: The Kabbalah Learning Centre, 1997).

Pema Chodron, *When Things Fall Apart.* (Boston: Shambala Classics, 1997).

Paulo Coelho, *The Alchemist.* (New York: HarperCollins/ HarperSanFrancisco, 1993).

Kathy Cordova, *Let Go / Let Miracles Happen: The Art of Spiritual Surrender.* (San Francisco: Conari Press, 2003).

Diane Drehler, *The Tao of Inner Peace*. (New York: Harper Perennial, 1990).

Gregg Drinkwater, Joshua Lesser, and David Shneer, *Torah Queeries: Weekly Commentaries on the Hebrew Bible*. (New York: New York University Press, 2009).

Piero Ferrucci, *The Power of Kindness*. (New York: Tarcher/Penguin, 2007).

Tzvi Freeman, *Bringing Heaven Down to Earth*. (Holbrook: Adams Media Corp., 1996).

Julie Galambush, *The Reluctant Parting*. (New York: HarperCollins/HarperSanFrancisco, 2005).

Louise Hay, *The AIDS Book: Creating a Positive Approach*. (Santa Monica: Hay House, 1988).

Rabbi Abraham Joshua Heschel, *I Asked for Wonder*. (Chestnut Ridge: The Crossroad Publishing Company, 2009).

Rabbi Abraham Joshua Heschel, *God In Search of Man*. (New York: Farrar, Straus, and Giroux, 1955).

Jeru Kabbal, *Finding Clarity: A Guide to the Deeper Levels of Your Being*. (Berkeley: North Atlantic Books, 2006).

Rabbi Lawrence Kushner, *God Was in This Place & I, i Did Not Know: Finding Self, Spirituality and Ultimate Meaning*. (New York: Jewish Lights Publishing, 1991).

Rabbi Alan Lew, *This is Real and You are Completely Unprepared: The Days of Awe as a Journey of Transformation*. (Boston: Little, Brown, and Company, 2003).

William Martin, *The Tao of Forgiveness: The Healing Power of Forgiving Others and Yourself*. (New York: Tarcher/Penguin, 2010).

Dan Millman, *The Laws of Spirit: A Tale of Transformation*. (Tiburon/ Novato: HK Kramer/New World Library, 1995).

Deng Ming-Dao, *365 Tao: Daily Meditations*. (New York: HarperSanFrancisco, 1992).

Deng Ming-Dao, *The Wandering Taoist*. (New York: Harper and Row, 1986).

Randy Pausch with Jeffrey Zaslow, *The Last Lecture*. (New York: Hyperion Books, 2008).

Jane Roberts, *Seth, Dreams and Projections of Consciousness*. (Manhasset: New Awareness Network, 1998).

Jane Roberts, *The Way Toward Health: A Seth Book*. (San Rafael: Amber-Allen Publishing, 1997).

Jane Roberts, *The Nature of Personal Reality: A Seth Book*. (Englewood Cliffs: Prentice-Hall, Inc., 1974).

Don Miguel Ruiz, *The Four Agreements*. (San Rafael: Amber-Allen Publishing, 1997).

Rabbi Rami Shapiro, *Tanya: the Masterpiece of Hasidic Wisdom.* (Woodstock: Skylight Paths Publishing, 2010).

Alyce Steadman, *Who's the Matter with Me?* (Marina del Rey: DeVorss Publications, 1966).

Dr. Ron Wolfson, *The Seven Questions You're Asked in Heaven.* (Woodstock: Jewish Lights Publishing, 2009).

Yeshiva of the Telshe Alumni, *The Quill of the Heart: The Jewish Approach to Human Relations.* (Suffern: Chofetz Chaim Heritage Foundation, 2nd Edition, 2003).

Endnotes

1   Printed by permission.

2   Marianne Williamson, *Forgiving Your Parents*, audiocassette, 11th tape in her series of lectures based on *A Course in Miracles* (New York: HarperCollins Publishers, 1992).

3   Ibid.

4   Printed by permission.

5   David Lieber (Senior Editor), *Etz Chaim, Torah and Commentary* (New York: The Rabbinical Assembly, The Jewish Publication Society, 2001), 69-70.

6   Ibid, 70.

7   Ibid, 1112.

8   Pia Mellody, with Andrea Wells Miller and J. Keith Miller, *Facing Codependence, What It Is, Where It Comes From, How It Sabotages Our Lives* (New York: Harper Collins/HarperSanFrancisco, 1989),143-146.

9   *The Holy Bible*, Second Edition (Nashville: Thomas Nelson Publishers, The Methodist Publishing House, 1963), 14.

10   Ibid, 59-60.

11   David Lieber (Senior Editor), *Etz Chaim, Torah and Commentary* (New York: The Rabbinical Assembly, The Jewish Publication Society, 2001), 652.

12   Printed by permission.

13   Ibid.

14   Lao Tzu, translated by Raymond Blakney, *The Way of Life, Tao Te Ching: A New Translation* (New York: Signet Classics, 1955), 63.

15   The Upside of Anger, directed by Mike Binder (2004; New Line Cinema, Los Angeles, CA: Warnerbrothersdvdmedia, 2005).

16   Amy-Jill Levine, Marc Zvi Brettler, Editors, *The Jewish Annotated New Testament* (New York: Oxford University Press, 2011), 10.

17   Louise L. Hay, *You Can Heal Your Life* (Carson: Hay House, 1984), 127-146.

18   Rabbi Steven Z. Leder, *The Extraordinary Nature of Ordinary Things* (Springfield: Behrman House, Inc., 1999), 3.

19   Printed by permission.

20   Amy-Jill Levine, Marc Zvi Brettler, Editors, *The Jewish Annotated New Testament* (New York: Oxford University Press, 2011), 137.

21   Rabbi Alan Lew, *One God Clapping: The Spiritual Path of a Zen Rabbi* (Woodstock: Jewish Lights Publishing, 2001), 49-50.

22   Rabbi Rami Shapiro, *Hasidic Tales, Annotated & Explained* (Woodstock: Skylight Paths Publishing, 2004), 178.

23   Rabbi Laurence Edwards, *"Change or Repetition?"* (Chicago: Rosh HaShanah D'var 5770, Or Chadash), reprinted by permission.

24   Rabbi Gershon Winkler, *Daily Kabbalah: Wisdom from the Tree of Life* (Berkeley: North Atlantic Books, 2004), 293.

25   *The Holy Bible*, Second Edition (Nashville: Thomas Nelson Publishers, The Methodist Publishing House, 1963), 49.

26   Richard Elliott Friedman, *Commentary on the Torah* (New York: HarperOne, 2001), 176.

27   Printed by permission.

28   *The Holy Bible,* Second Edition (Nashville: Thomas Nelson Publishers, The Methodist Publishing House, 1963), 499.

29   Printed by permission.

30   Marianne Williamson, *Forgiving Your Parents*, audiocassette, 11th tape in her series of lectures based on *A Course in Miracles* (New York: HarperCollins Publishers, 1992).

31   Rabbi Simkha Y. Weintraub, *Healing of Soul, Healing of Body: Spiritual Leaders Unfold the Strength and Solace in Psalms* (Woodstock: Jewish Lights Publishing, 1994), 18.

32   Printed by permission.

33   Printed by permission.

34   Daniel Matt, *The Essential Kabbalah: The Heart of Jewish Mysticism* (Edison: Castle Books, 1995), 99.

35   Daniel Matt, *God & The Big Bang: Discovery Harmony Between Science & Spirituality* (Woodstock: Jewish Lights Publishing, 1996), 171.

36   Printed by permission.

37   Marianne Williamson, *Forgiving Your Parents*, audiocassette, 11th tape in her series of lectures based on *A Course in Miracles* (New York: HarperCollins Publishers, 1992).

38   Alan Morinis, *Everyday Holiness, The Jewish Spiritual Path of Mussar* (Boston: Shambhala Publications, Inc., 2007), 109.

39   Rabbi David A. Cooper, *God Is a Verb: Kabbalah and the Practice of Mystical Judaism* (New York: Riverhead Books, 1997), 243-244.

40   David Lieber (Senior Editor), *Etz Chaim, Torah and Commentary* (New York: The Rabbinical Assembly, The Jewish Publication Society, 2001), 4.

41   Linda Pastan, "For a Parent," *Kol Haneshamah: Mahzor Leyamim Nora'im* (Elkins Park: Reconstructionist Press, 1999), 1022.

42   "Anonymous Poem," *Kol Haneshamah: Mahzor Leyamim Nora'im* (Elkins Park: Reconstructionist Press, 1999), 1023.

43   David Lieber (Senior Editor), *Etz Chaim, Torah and Commentary* (New York: The Rabbinical Assembly, The Jewish Publication Society, 2001), 4.

44   Amy-Jill Levine, Marc Zvi Brettler, Editors, *The Jewish Annotated New Testament* (New York: Oxford University Press, 2011), 16.

45   Rabbi Rami Shapiro, *Hasidic Tales, Annotated & Explained* (Woodstock: Skylight Paths Publishing, 2004), 178.

46   Rabbi Gershon Winkler, *Daily Kabbalah: Wisdom from the Tree of Life* (Berkeley: North Atlantic Books, 2004), 111.

47   Rabbi Joseph Telushkin, *Jewish Wisdom: Ethical, Spiritual, and Historical Lessons from the Great Works and Thinkers* (New York: William Morrow & Co., 1994), 67.

48   Dr. Abraham Joshua Heschel with Carl Stern, *A Conversation with the Late Dr. Abraham Heschel* (NBC News, program no. 205, aired February 4, 1973).

49   Ibid.

50   *The Holy Bible*, Second Edition (Nashville: Thomas Nelson Publishers, The Methodist Publishing House, 1963), 1-2.

51   Rabbi Moshe Weissman, *The Midrash Says, The Book of Beraishis* (Brooklyn: Benei Yakov Publications, 1980), 454.

Made in the USA
San Bernardino, CA
18 March 2014